LIVE FOODS

Natures Perfect System of

Human Nutrition

192 RECIPES

by

George & Doris Fathman

The Ehret Literature Publishing Company, Inc.
P O Box 24
Dobbs Ferry, New York 10522-0024
www.arnoldehret.org

Seventh Edition

ISBN 1-884772-03-X

Printed in the United States of America

George and Doris Fathman

This book is dedicated with deep gratitude to the memory of the late Professor Arnold Ehret, one of the world's greatest benefactors, originator of the Mucusless Diet Healing System.

GEORGE and DORIS FATHMAN

Authors

CONTENTS

Introduction

What would Arnold Ehret the great German nutritionist, philosopher and visionary who wrote his books about one hundred years ago, say if he walked into a supermarket of a big city.

He would walk up and down the many aisles, past the ten thousands of different bottles, boxes, packages, cans and plastic containers, the tubes and jars, the colorful, attractive displays, watch the smiling, pretty, young faces on the labels, pick up an item here and there, and read the fantastic claims of brand X and Y. Finally he would throw up his arms and explain in a mixture of horror and amazement: "And where is the food?"

Eventually, he would find his way to the produce section in a corner of the supermarket, pick up one of those shiny apples or one of those waxed oranges, hold them to his nose and wonder: "who did the makeup on the fruit? It has no fragrance." Ending up purchasing a few tomatoes, Ehret would bite into one and immediately burst into song: "Where has all the flavor gone!" A mushy, watery, tasteless, nutritionless, genetically modified, red little ball of bluff.

By that time, our traveler in time, hopefully, will find his way to a much smaller, <u>natural</u> food store, shaking his head why people "progressed" in the 20th Century to building so many unnatural foodless stores.

Arnold Ehret struggled with serious health challenges as a young man, cured himself after having been given up by his doctors and left a legacy of self-empowering, health promoting ways of eating in his classic books "The Mucusless Diet Healing System" and "Rational Fasting" as well as other writings.

Forty years after Ehret died, a couple living in California, George and Doris Fathman discovered the teachings of the German nutritionist, cured themselves of major health afflictions, and wrote a book: *Live Foods. Nature's Perfect System of Human Nutrition*; which built upon Arnold Ehret's foundational work and presented a very pragmatic, easy to follow Ehret in everyday life approach to eating with 192 recipes.

It is a raw food un-cookbook with a few transitional recipes since Ehret advocated a firm, but gentle path towards eating exclusively "Live Foods".

Itself a classic in the 1960s and 1970s, the Fathman's "Live Foods" book went out of print for a while until the publishers decided to make this gem, which predates a plethora of raw food preparation appearing in recent years, again available to a larger audience and practitioners.

Today, the raw food movement has gained an enormous momentum and enthusiastic practitioners gather at festivals and conferences in many countries.

There are rawfood restaurants in many cities, raw food spas and retreats like the "Optimum Health Institutes" in San Diego, California and Austin, Texas; the "Hippocrates Health Institute" in Florida. Many people enjoy the raw way of eating not only for reasons of health and longevity and vitality, but also for the unrefined and yet very sophisticated pleasures of superior flavor, more subtle textures, shorter preparation time, less exposure to negative radiations from unhealthful cooking devices like microwave ovens, easier transportation and storage, longer shelf-life. Raw food has become the ultimate eating experience, the choice of the natural gourmet, as well as a most powerful therapeutic tool for the self-responsible, active health seeker.

It has become clear today that all other diets essentially have failed, especially the weight-loss fad diets which have a long-term success rate of less than 5%. Optimal weight for every person is a sure "side effect" of raw food. The fruit contains the right enzymes, the right vitamins in ideal proportions. The vegetables are the bodybuilders and sustain the body with truly absorbable minerals which is rarely the case with synthetic substitutes. The nuts and sprouts provide easily assimilable protein. In short, why would anyone take "beneficial designer drugs" concocted in the chemical factories, dispensed in little pills, with no way of sensory evaluation of the substance by our natural food selection organs, the taste buds, and the olfactory sense, when the fresh fruit, the colorful vegetables tells us very well as we see them, chew them, whether they are agreeable to us or not. This rather recent invention of the gustatory bypass where we swallow something totally tasteless in capsules or even inject substances via I.V. directly into the bloodstream is actually a horrifying invalidation and ultimately a devastating expropriation of our natural organs of perception which have evolved over billions of years.

III

Trust your nose again, let your tongue assess the necessary daily requirements, let your eyes be attracted again by organically grown, unadulterated, genuine freshness of food as it becomes available at reasonable prices in the changes of the season. Soon you will select again what is good for you and judge the offerings of nature with the regained clarity and certainty of unperverted tastebuds.

You will eat to enjoy the build the power to do what you want to do instead of constantly worrying whether you get enough of this or that. You will be no longer the terrified victim of the politics of food fears constantly compensating for heavily advertised "dangers of deficiencies" – you are getting enough of substance A, B, C, D, E, etc.? Serious individual imbalances notwithstanding, most "deficiencies" are caused by the over processing, over-refining, natural food products, and then adding toxic artificial preservatives, artificial flavoring, artificial coloring. When you ingest these dead, adultered nutritional insults, usually masked with strong sugar, salt or spice stimulants to trick your taste buds, you burden your body which mobilizes internal resources to compensate, but only for a limited time, then degenerative processes take you down on the long road of pain, more pill and eventually surgery and serious disease. The inevitable dramatic and traumatic emergency interventions provide in most cases only temporary relief, because they still do not deal with the fundamental underlying non-negotiable laws of nature.

Not for millennia, but for millions of years, the co-evolutionary processes of plant life and human development have sustained the continually of life and have provided thousands of generations willing to respect and obey the ecological cycles and interactions with a natural perfect system of human nutrition.

Those who cleanse the body temple and nourish it with foods in their natural state in reasonable quantities will infallibly increase their vitality, their longevity, sense of well being, and above all experience levels of sustained joy and happiness otherwise unimaginable.

More and more people lost their faith in the pharmaceutical companies' ability to provide the magic bullet, the miracle pill or even the truly effective problem solving quick fix. It is becoming increasingly clear that the many diseases with ever new names are advancing faster than the methods to stop them the microbes develop resistance to yesterday's shotgun antibiotic than the laboratories turn out the latest antidote. The critics who voice their well-founded opposition against the frantic, profit-driven chemical, technological race against nature, against the wars and battles "advanced", "developed", countries wage against the signals and symptoms which are nature's way of indicating false "progress", "solutions" leading to greater problems, are reaching a wider and wider audience.

George and Doris Fathman were not medical conventional doctors or chemists or scientists, but they were able to heal themselves as many others who followed the natural laws of nutrition as advocated by Arnold Ehret or Shelton or Tilden or Gandhi or Gabriel Cousens or Victoria Boutenko or Viktoras Kulvinskas or Ann Wigmore. The results are in, based on thousand fold experience not to be dismissed anymore as "anecdotes". Life experience does not need the validation of a "scientific" ideology. It is the other way around. The self-responsible health seeker will not wait until doctrines change and cannot wait when caring for and about those suffering in these moments. The health seeker will move towards self-empowerment and become a health-builder who will stop putting toxins into the body, cleanse the system of old poisons, exercise, breathe fresh air and above all fuel the body with the best, with the perfect vitality source ever created at any given time: Live Foods: Nature's truly perfect system of human nutrition.

Now all that is needed is a trip to the organic produce section in a good natural food store and a spirit of exploration as the delicious, delightful 192 different recipes in this book will restore the vim and vigor of your life-forces while you progress from fast food to instant real food delivered in its perfect edible package, for example: a fresh fragrant apple, pear, peach, date, fig . . . .

You are getting hungry?

Help yourself . . .

To the gifts of nature.

Toronto, August 2002

Prof. Dr. Ludwig Max Fischer

PREFACE TO FIFTH PRINTING

So many people have written us telling about their experiences on the raw food regime recommended in this book and how much good it has done them that they want to know when we are going to publish another. In our opinion there is no necessity for another book. This one has all the basic principles you need, and we don't want to deny you the thrill of using your own imagination to improve on our suggestions.

Since the first printing of our book many people have written us asking if we are still on the raw food program and how we are faring on it. To all inquirers we enthusiastically reply that we still are, and after nearly nine years we are more sold on it than when we began. And we are faring beautifully.

We have not yet reached the goal of the 100% fruitarian regime we mentioned on page 28, but are working towards it. We are still about 90% along the way. It is an uphill battle, but we have no intention of giving up.

On our eight month lecture tour covering 11,000 miles from Vancouver to San Diego a few years ago we met several fruitarians in Escondido, California, one man who had lived for 45 years on this regime, and another couple who had been on it for many years, also in Escondido. But this part of the country has a year round mild climate and is in the very center of the organic producing area of the west coast.

Our biggest problem since moving to Show Low in August last year has been getting adequate supplies of fresh fruit. So we have to compromise with vegetables and greens, along with nuts, seeds and dried fruit.

But Show Low has so many advantages over Tucson (where we lived when we put out the first three printings) that we don't mind. It's a small town (2,500 population) in the White Mountains (6,400 ft. elevation), surrounded by pine forests, where the air is crystal clear, smog-free, the water is pure and the atmosphere invigorating. We feel it's next door to heaven, and are most grateful to be privileged to live and work here.

Let me assure the readers of this book that while raw food is a wonderful aid to regaining and maintaining good health, it is no 'cure-all'. If you have bodily conditions that require medical attention, by all means avail yourself of it. Incidentally, there have been some fantastic advances in chiropractic science in the last few years, and on the basis of our own experience and that of many of our friends we heartily recommend it for your consideration.

My hay fever that I mentioned on page 4 has vanished, although I do have occasional cleansing crises. But they don't last long and my energy and drive are just as strong as ever.

One thing we have proven to ourselves is that we can survive on raw food in a winter climate. In Tucson where we lived for ten years and the winters are mild, staying on raw food was no problem. But in Show Low the winters sometimes get pretty rugged. We had three days of 36 below last January and quite a few days of below zero, but we experienced no difficulty with our raw food program.

On our lecture tour it surprised us to learn that many raw fooders did not have optimum health, for either one or both of these reasons: they were unhappy with their life situation or spiritually out of joint. In either of these cases, raw food is no panacea. You can eat the best in the world, but if you are mad at your wife, husband, job, government, or whatever, you are going to suffer some type of psychosomatic disease symptom. This tends to make you overeat and become a "foodaholic," like too much liquor makes an alcoholic—just as deadly an escape mechanism.

Likewise, if you don't enjoy a reverent, loving and dependent relationship with your Creator, you will have a hidden spiritual as well as physical hunger. As we stress in our book, health is threefold—body, soul and spirit.

Many folks have written us, and some even called long distance, to ask if we still use and advise the taking of vitamins and minerals. With the horrible deterioration of our food supply, our answer is emphatically yes, now more than ever. But be sure you get an organic source of supply.

Hidden hunger is another bugaboo bothering many on the raw food program. Organic vitamins and minerals help in this area, but let's face it, even with the regular use of these aids, if you can't get organically raised food **year round,** you are going to have a certain amount of hidden hunger, especially when you have reached an advanced biological age such as ours and have started on the raw food program only recently.

Do you know when you should begin on raw foods? At birth. The many children we have seen who have been nurtured that way don't have hidden hunger, are healthy, well behaved and a credit to their parents. With us old folks it's another matter.

So many have written us and asked us during our lecture tour about what to eat when they go to restaurants that we can't keep track of the number. It seems to be a universal problem, and we have it too, so we can sympathize with them. Even those who are 100% raw fooders and thrive on it don't seem to know what to do when they have to eat out.

Well, our answer is to go to cafeterias or smorgasbords. In a cafeteria or smorgasbord restaurant you most always have a large selection of salads that are nourishing and satisfying. When traveling, prepare your own food and eat lightly between major stops.

A two-pronged problem our correspondents compain about is what to serve their guests; and what to eat when they are invited out. In your own home, you have an abundance of selections from the recipes in this book which should satisfy the most demanding palate, and provide an unusual taste thrill to boot — setting the hostess apart as a most remarkable "cook"! When you are invited out, tell your hostess you are on a special diet ordered by your doctor, then suggest any of the easy to prepare recipes from our book. Being gracious and diplomatic is most always in order, and you don't irritate friends and relatives unnecessarily.

With food prices now going through the roof because of artificially created scarcities, we strongly recommend you look into the dehydration of fruits and vegetables for easy storage.

One can survive a long time on dried food, as the Indians and many primitive tribes throughout the world have proven. There are several dehydrators on the market, and men who are handy with tools can build their own fairly inexpensively.

We have had many requests to publish "Live Foods" in paperback. The cheaper price puts it in reach of everyone. We have a bushel basket of testimonials from grateful folks who say this raw food program has been of inestimable value to them. Some have even said it saved their lives.

We are extremely grateful and happy that Ehret Literature Publishing Company has taken over the publishing of the book. In view of our dedication of "Live Foods" to the revered memory of Prof. Arnold Ehret, it is most appropriate that his publisher thinks well enough of our work to include it in his list of Ehret classics.

After nine years now of being on and off of the raw food program, my wife and I are more than ever convinced that it is the only rational diet for man. We most enthusiastically recommend you give it a serious trial.

Many thousands enjoy better health because of the teachings of Prof. Arnold Ehret, originator of the Mucusless Diet Healing System, to whom so many owe so much.

We agree wholeheartedly with the judgment of him by the late Dr. Benedict Lust, M.D., ie.

"Prof. Ehret will get the largest following a diet expert could have. His system is the only genuine solution of the dietetic problem. He has given us more information than all other experts combined."

G. F.

Dear kitchen slave. What a way to address you! Yet virtually every woman who has a family, and many who don't, is literally held slave to her stove. Some love it; others hate it.

Have you ever wondered if there were some way to rid yourself of the chains binding you to that kitchen of yours as you shop for the latest in TV dinners? Well, there is, so be of good cheer, and read on.

You will be delighted to discover, if you have the courage to follow the no cooking system, that you will spend at least one-half as much time in your kitchen. I'm sure it does not tax your imagination to visualize the many enjoyable activities you would rather engage in instead of the hours spent preparing meals and cleaning up the mess afterwards.

Very likely the most valuable blessing from following this system is the dramatic improvement in your health and that of your family—a priceless boon no money can buy, no doctor, drug or hospital can bestow.

There are other bonuses too. You will find your food bill cut a minimum of one-half, probably much more. Could you use the money saved for other expenses?

Health Has Many Facets

There are many factors to achieving total health, which we define as:

HEALTH FOR THE BODY

BEAUTY FOR THE SOUL

TRUTH FOR THE SPIRIT

Some of them are: positive thinking, high moral and ethical principles, congenial and profitable work, fresh air and water, exercise, doing all things in moderation, and spiritual aspirations. But proper diet, in our view, forms the foundation stone on which the superstructure of your life and ours must be built. It is the first step on a long journey.

A house can be only as good as the foundation on which it stands. What kind of a life can be lived when the body is sick and diseased? Only a sick and diseased life—physically, emotionally, mentally and spiritually.

As we look about us what do we see? A world so sick and famished it seems almost on the point of extinction. Have you ever noticed that many of the rulers of the world's governments and corporations are sick men who die prematurely, as a rule? Is there a way out of this tragic condition? We believe there is, and that belief is backed up by our personal experience and that of thousands of folks who have faithfully followed the live foods program.

How This Book Was Born

Perhaps you may be interested to learn how this unusual little book came into being. There aren't many like it, you know. You could count them on the fingers of your two hands. But you will see more and more of them in the years to come.

A couple of years ago my wife was besieged by our friends to give them the recipes for the "fascinating, unusual and delicious meals they had when guests in our home. Doris would say, "Oh, I follow some of John Martin Reinecke's recipes, but mostly I just make them up out of my head." Then the incredulous ladies would reply, "But how can you prepare these meals without recipes? How do you know what proportions to use?"

Then Doris would say, "I just use a dash of this and a dash of that." Many women, of course, follow such a haphazard method, but when you are asked for a recipe, just saying a dash of this and a dash of that isn't very satisfactory.

The next step was a request by our inquisitive friends for Doris to start a "cooking" class on the no cooking system so they could watch her and see how she did it. The response was enthusiastic, but soon died out. Why? Because the folks were usually so sick, or members of their families were whom they had to nurse, that they couldn't come to class! So, to satisfy the desires and needs of an ever increasing circle of inquirers for recipes with exact proportions, we have published this book.

At this point you may be wondering how we came to adopt the live foods program. Have we been on it all our lives or is it a late acquisition? If I may be pardoned the personal reference, and in the fervent hope my story may help a fellow sufferer avoid the unnecessary agonies caused by dietary ignorance, following is the account of how this book was born.

The Hay Fever Scourge

In 1950 we moved from Chicago to Oregon. In 1951 I began to develop the classic symptoms of "hay fever." There is no need to give the details of this dread scourge. Anyone who suffers from it knows the tortures of the damned. I had lived in Chicago, the hay fever capital of the country, for twenty-five years and never once had had a touch of it. Yet here I was living out in "God's Country" on the banks of the beautiful Rogue River, and I began to manifest all the symptoms. It didn't make sense. I went to the best doctors, tried every pill, potion and diet they recommended, and kept getting worse and worse.

In 1952 we moved to San Francisco, where my hay fever increased in intensity. By 1956 it became so severe it seemed as if I were going to have to abandon my profession of court reporting because I couldn't blow my nose every minute on the minute and operate my Stenograph at the same time. Splitting headaches plagued me constantly. Seldom a day passed I didn't take from one to five Anacin. For the last three years I've been on the live food regime I don't know what the word headache means.

We Discover Prof. Ehret's Teachings

It was in 1956 that Larry La Barre, our good friend in Mt. View, California, introduced us to the late Prof. Arnold Ehret's book, "The Mucusless Diet Healing System." Ehret's radical and revolutionary theories intrigued us immensely. The foundation of his work rests on gradually replacing cooked (or dead) food with raw (or live) food — with the ultimate goal of an exclusively fruitarian program. Several of our friends on the peninsula reported excellent results from following the Ehret system, so we decided to give it a try.

For the first few months everything went fine. But then we began to get subtle yet persistent cravings to go back to the "flesh pots of Egypt." Occasionally we would sneak in a hamburger, cheese, potatoes, so on. Before we realized what had happened we found ourselves back on our old cooking regime we had followed for a lifetime, and Ehret went out the window.

However, the memory of the benefits that accrued from our experience with the live food regime persisted, so we tried to go on it once more. With no better luck than before, we gave it up again.

In 1960 we moved to Tucson, Arizona. For a short time the dry desert climate seemed to help my hay fever. Then all of a sudden it played a return engagement, with more brutality than ever before. This was truly a desperate situation that had me hanging on the ropes, not knowing which way to turn for help.

Journey's End

In the spring of 1964 at times I would be literally choking, unable to breathe through either the nose or mouth. One night the attack became so severe I distinctly heard the Grim Reaper knocking at my door, saying, "This is it, boy, give up the ghost."

As I had no intention of acceding to his summons, I said, "Nuts to you. I'll fight this insidious ailment to the bitter end."

At that moment it indeed seemed like the bitter end, but an angel in the disguise of my beloved and devoted wife came to my rescue as an answer to deep prayer. She was inspired to work on my feet, with her knowledge of foot relaxation therapy, and brought me out of the spasm that threatened my demise. Within minutes I could breathe, and lay relaxed on the bed.

Then it was while giving thanks to God for sparing my life that I seemed to hear an inner voice tell me the only salvation for my nearly fatal condition was to return to the live food program I had twice before espoused and given up.

In passing I must give credit for the great help received from Pearl Johnson, Tucson's outstanding reflexologist. Several months of her zone therapy treatments relieved many of the tensions created by years of accumulated body toxins. If you are fortunate to have a good zone therapist where you live, much help can be given your body that cannot be achieved with any other modality of treatment. Pearl also did wonders for Doris in pulling her out of a serious condition.

Clouds Have Silver Linings

On June 1, 1964, I told Doris that this time I was going to resume live foods that very day and stay on them, be the consequences what they may, that if I were going to die I might as well die on live food as cooked, that I felt was my only salvation.

For the following three years that we have been on the no cooking program we have been tempted on and off, as we were before, to go off the diet, but on the whole we have stuck to it pretty faithfully, with the result that my hay fever condition has cleared up about 99%. I feel certain that in another year or two it will have completely vanished, never more to return.

Three months after starting on the live food program in 1964 I had lost 35 lbs. of unneeded and unwanted blubber, resulting in a sharp upward zooming of energy and work capacity. Many a day have I worked hard for 18 hours, with no fatigue. And so has Doris. At times I have felt such an upsurge of energy it seemed I hardly had any body weight and that I would have to go outdoors and run in order to work off the excess energy, or else climb the mountain just behind our home. Of course I didn't give in to this urge, although I probably should have. At any rate, at my present age of sixty I often experience these feelings of physical elation, and I know that as my body becomes ever cleaner they will become permanent.

We Meet John Martin Reinecke

While my gratitude goes first to Prof. Ehret for his magnificent contribution of introducing natural methods to me, I must in all fairness give due credit to John Martin Reinecke, N.D., D.B.M. (American fruit originator, explorer and raw food expert), for returning steadfastly my interest back to the wonders and importance of 100% raw foods. It was my constant reading of his marvelous articles published each month in a health magazine under the heading, "Adventures in Raw Foods," that whetted my appetite to resume the live food regime that has given me the vibrant health I now enjoy.

At Christmas time in 1964 we had the privilege of visiting Mr. Reinecke at his home and learning from him first hand many of the secrets of his success in promoting the raw food program. There were many things he told us that we had read in his articles, but to hear it from his own lips was inspiring and bolstered our determination to stay on the program of raw foods.

We were fortunate to be invited to a Christmas dinner prepared by Mr. Reinecke and his ardent raw food devotee and helper, Bob Parfet, an architect who had miraculously regained his total health through 100% raw foods. It was the most delicious Christmas dinner we had ever eaten, one which makes us drool even yet when we think of it. We were privileged to watch them prepare this raw food feast, so we could go home and do likewise — which you can be sure we did.

As an interesting side topic during this unusual raw food meal Mr. Reinecke told us how he had prepared a seven course raw food banquet in San Diego, California, for 200 people. It consisted of raw tomato soup, raw celery-nut-meat loaf, chili pepper sauce, raw gravy, cucumber-onion salads, raw apple-banana pie with coconut topping, and the enthusiastic response was overwhelming.

Then Mr. Reinecke explained why raw fooders sometimes seem to be always hungry when starting on raw foods, as follows:

"In the beginning, when changing over from dead cooked foods to live on raw foods, many raw food beginners' bodies have been so starved and depleted for the want of good live foods that they seem never to be able to get enough of these delicious and nourishing raw things. Therefore for a period of time in making the change-over, they seem to be always hungry and eating continually. It is a hang-over deficiency disease caused only by their past mistakes of eating cooked foods. But this hunger does not last forever. It is not because the raw foods are not satisfying. It is because the body has such great need for the raw things it has been deprived of and missing for years. By instinct a raw fooder soon learns to eat all the raw foods he wants, but knows exactly when to stop before overeating. He stops when he could still eat a little bit more but doesn't because he is satisfied but not stuffed. In this way he is always able to keep his keen sense of appetite for food at all times as natural, normal and healthy creatures do. A raw fooder can **always** eat, and this is the way it should be.

"Also it is true that raw foods digest quicker and easier than cooked foods ever did. This sometimes makes the beginner feel that he must eat more often, although he shouldn't necessarily. It usually does not matter how much or how often a new raw fooder may eat as long as his body craves it and the particular raw food agrees with him. In due time as his body becomes well nourished and satisfied with the raw foods, he will gradually taper off to less food and eat less often. He will then have more health, strength and faith in raw foods. He will find that it takes only three average sized raw food meals a day to satisfy him—sometimes perhaps even less. But if he is on a liquid diet of raw foods such as only raw juices, then in this case he will drink six or more glasses of liquid raw food a day, until he returns to three or less solid raw food meals a day."

"Of the many thousands of raw food students that I have known, I also know that their likes and dislikes for certain raw foods may vary just as much so. I think everyone who begins raw foods should always eat only those raw foods that he likes best and those that agree with him most. I do not believe in eating a raw food that is distasteful just because it may be good for one. Eat it because you like it, and it agrees with you! If you find a particular raw food that you crave, then eat plenty of it as long as it agrees, because there is something in it that your body needs. Make a complete meal of any desired raw food until you become tired of it, then find something else you want that is raw.

"Unsprayed food is best when it is organically grown, of course, but organic or not organically raised, if it is washed well, all food is better eaten raw than cooked. Most important is to eat whatever one eats 100% raw, because that is the real secret of total health and longevity. It is not always possible for everyone to obtain his food free from sprays and chemical fertilizers. Therefore, he must be practical and do the next thing best. If you must eat supermarket produce, then wash it thoroughly and eat it raw. Cooking does not neutralize the poisons—it only doubles it, so at least eat it raw. Yes, one can live entirely on organically raised produce best, but ordinarily it is too expensive and inconvenient for the average person to get such food. When traveling over the country at times I have had to eat the raw fruits and vegetables bought in the supermarkets, but even so I lived a much better life, free from pain and sickness by eating it washed and raw than if I had cooked it.

"In all of my 25 years of maintaining myself in excellent health on total raw foods, I have never been cursed with a hidden hunger feeling, nor a lack of nourishing raw food. Raw foods have always kept me free from jungle fevers and deadly diseases at home, including cancer, by faithfully remaining on the raw food program. In my advanced years I am still full of vim, vigor and vitality equal to a man half my age. For a sick man who was given up to die by his best medical doctors more than two decades ago, you had better believe me! —that 100% raw foods are best, and they did it!

Crazy Appetites

"Sometimes it takes about a year to adjust completely to raw foods. As an illustration, when I lived in Los Angeles, California, while I was on my first attempt of the Richter program of raw foods, I woke up one night out of a sound sleep with an insatiable appetite for Mexican food, which I had never eaten in my entire life. We had none in the house, of course, but the desire was so over-powering that I had to look all over town to find a restaurant where I could satisfy it. And at 1:30 in the morning that isn't easy! But find it I did, and after I had had my fill of good Mexican raw Guacamole (mashed avocado) salad with raw fresh hot chili pepper sauce, I went back to bed and slept soundly. Later I found out that it was the natural raw capsicum contained in the fresh peppers that was the missing trace element my body craved. My good friend, George Fathman, now tells me that he also had almost exactly the same experience in San Jose, California.

"This demonstrates the recurring crises a person on the live food program might sometimes endure until he completely cleanses his blood stream, which takes approximately one year. The live food stirs up the hornet's nest of toxins created by years of ingesting dead food. In the process of ridding the body of these toxins oftentimes artifical hungers are aroused, as well as intense desires for the foodless foods previously indulged. These storms are difficult to endure, but once they pass, as pass they inevitably do, the body acquires a new burst of energy and well-being. As wave after wave of these cleansing crises deluge the live fooder, he wonders whether it is worthwhile. Then it is that he needs a good well balanced raw food menu-guide and the encouragement of older and more experienced live fooders to bolster his courage and determination. For it is then, when the going is hard, that the temptation to give up and return to the old way of eating is strongest and easiest to give in to. Especially if you have a tribe of Job's Comforters in your family circle who let you know in no uncertain terms their doubts about your sanity. George Fathman and I think that perhaps it would be well to start an organization called 'Foods Anonymous,' similar to Alcoholics Anonymous, to provide encouragement and sound advice in these few periods of trial and crisis.

"So remember that hidden hunger is a disease from a past life of wrong eating habits that comes only from cooked foods. Then when beginning raw foods and you seem always hungry, don't forget that it is a hang-over! Sometimes it is not detected until a well balanced raw food diet brings it out and heals it in due time."

Aside from the obvious reason that hidden hunger **seems** to be caused (although it is not) by raw food being digested in approximately half the time of cooked food (in which time **it is**), I felt there must be a more compelling reason for this condition, because even eating five or six times a day did not dispel it. (It takes time—it took many years to get sick on cooked foods, so why expect raw foods to heal so quickly? It just doesn't work that way, because nature works slowly but surely.) For a working person, five or six meals a day is difficult to manage (and in reality it is very unnecessary.)

After much pondering on this problem, one day an answer seemed to formulate itself. Perhaps it was because of the ever increasing poisoning of our food supply through insecticides and chemical fertilizers each year—a factor Ehret never had to contend with, as it came into being long after his time. We may be getting the necessary bulk and **some** nourishment, but not the necessary **complete nourishment** from what we buy in the supermarket. And as it is almost impossible for most of us to live 100% on organically raised food, maybe the solution lies in eating along with the raw foods organically raised food supplements in the form of natural vitamins and minerals—which we used to get more abundantly in our food, but no more.

Food Supplements

I had tried vitamins by the bucketful down through the years, with no results of a lasting nature. But they were not organically produced vitamins. Also I had not gone through the vitally necessary cleansing regime of a sustained 100% live food program. So, recently we began eating organically produced vitamin food supplements, and what a revelation! No more "hidden hunger," and an actual decrease in the amount of food intake. No more between-meals snacks needed, no more abnormal appetites, nor five or six meals a day—only one or two, often times just one.

To those of you who may already be on the live food regime and are annoyed at being constantly hungry, with that "not quite satisfied" feeling, we suggest you try eating an organically produced vitamin supplement, and see if that doesn't help you, as it has helped us.

Perhaps some people get a better supply of produce from their markets over the country than we do in Arizona, for we seem to have to take some natural vitamin supplements. Then also, some people make frequent trips to the fabulous open market in Tijuana just across the Mexican border, where they get many organically raised fruits and vegetables. But as for us, we have found that the raw food program, along with vitamin and mineral supplements, very beneficial, and we hope that you may too. At least it won't cost you overly much and it may be worth giving it a try. It certainly can't harm you.

Cleanse the Temple

At this point, let me emphasize the fact that, as Prof. Ehret tells us, while proper food is indeed important, there is another factor of far greater importance in acquiring health. And that is: removing the obstructions in the body, the mucus, the toxins, the waste material, the poisons, call them by whatever name you choose. The rather ugly name for it, which everyone knows only too well, is constipation. But Ehret tells us that this is a constipation of not only the colon, but EVERY CELL IN THE BODY—a far different concept than we normally conceive, but sadly only too true. As you soon discover when you begin the cleansing program.

Vibrant energy results from having a clean body, internally more than externally, more than it does from stuffing it with food, even the best of food. After you have been on the live food cleansing regime for a while you will be amazed at the unbelievable stench and filth excreted from your organs of elimination, even the skin, sometimes almost unbearable. At such times you realize what a "pressure cooker" you have been living with in your mid-section all your life, and you will marvel how you have managed to survive as long as you have. You will understand then how you and I have defiled the sacred temple of the living God. And it is only to the extent we cleanse the rubbish from the temple that the Spirit of God can manifest in us to do His will on earth as it is in Heaven.

Remember the old saying: "Cleanliness is next to Godliness." In our view, it should read: "Cleanliness is a prerequisite to Godliness."

Even though I had studied deeply in the health field ever since 1935, attending dozens of lectures by recognized "authorities" and reading countless books, not a single one revealed this great liberating secret to me until I found Ehret. It is the finest talisman you will ever possess with which to unlock the gates to your body temple of exhilarating health.

Kitchen Drudgery Emancipation

Now that I've delivered myself of the "how" this book came to be, let me delve briefly into the "why." The live food program has done wonders for our health, our pocketbook and our time. It has emancipated Doris from most of her kitchen drudgery. And we earnestly desire to share these blessings with others who are searching as we did for the elusive goal of health. It constantly amazes us to witness the absolute poverty of understanding of these things that to us are "old hat," so to speak. When we mention live foods being our sole source of nutrition people look at us as if we had announced we just landed from Mars, and with about as much belief.

In the short space of this book we can't possibly give all the many factors that have contributed to our health and vitality. All we can do is drop a few hints that we hope will be helpful to you to encourage you to pursue your own study and research. We can't emphasize too strongly there is no such animal as an "authority" <u>unless and until you prove it in your own experience.</u> Keep constantly in mind this motto: the test of truth is, does it work?

For example. Some authorities maintain a good nourishing breakfast will give you the start for the day you need; other authorities say this is the bunk, that what you should do is eat no breakfast. So, what do you do in a case like this? Test their conflicting theories in your experience, and life itself will give you the correct answer — for YOU — which is all that is important. Don't concern yourself whether the correct answer for you differs from that for someone else. We are all different, and the old adage still holds true: one man's food may be another man's poison, figuratively speaking, that is.

An instance in point. Doris loves green peppers —I despise them. She can eat them by the bucketful. If I eat one tiny slice it will back up on me for two days. Yet all the diet experts tell you to eat lots of green peppers, that they are loaded with vitamin C. Eat what agrees with you and don't worry about what the experts say.

This problem of contradictory advice presented itself in my own case in many ways. For years I followed the hearty breakfast advice, and felt completely miserable. After trying the no breakfast regime, I felt far better. My breakfast now consists of a brisk walk down the hill every morning to get the paper, with vigorous deep breathing exercises going down and back up the hill. It's the best breakfast I ever had in my life, and puts me in the pink of condition for the day's work. Seldom do I get hungry before noon, and by then I have a good appetite.

Which brings to mind a cardinal health rule that, if faithfully followed, will do wonders for the well-being of your body: eat only when you feel hungry, not because the clock says it's meal time. You will be astounded at how much you will cut down on your food intake, how much better your body will feel. And your pocketbook too.

When I mentioned this principle to a friend, he said: "Well, that wouldn't work with me. I'd have to eat only one meal a day, which means I'd be eating all day long, for I'm always hungry!" But from my observation, very few people eat to satisfy genuine hunger. In most cases it's a matter of habit resulting from the false idea that we need "three square meals a day."

Why not experiment for a week or two and skip a meal or so when you don't actually feel genuinely hungry. You won't die—at least not right away! It might surprise you to discover how a short fast now and then will overcome a lot of stomach upsets, bilious conditions and what not—plus creating a really good appetite for your next meal. It will be an enlightening experience for you, and rewarding too.

The Cook Book Craze

We realize many women will use this book to adorn their tables with these, to them, new, exciting and unusual dishes with which to wow their friends. For that seems to be a never ending search among culinary artists—judging from the vast number of cook books in book stores, with a new one making its appearance every week or so. However, if you want to really derive the maximum benefits from this no cooking system, it requires loyalty, faithfulness, determination, and above all courage to stick to it, come what may.

Remember the story of grandpa. Down on the farm they had a flash flood. A guest of the woman of the house was watching the raging waters rushing five feet deep over the yard when all of a sudden she spied a straw hat going along with the stream. She didn't think anything was unusual about that until she saw the hat reverse direction and go against the current. After several such sorties she asked her host if she had any explanation for such an odd phenomenon.

"Oh," she replied, "that's grandpa. He said yesterday come hell or high water he was going to mow the lawn today."

The Good Old American Diet

One question we know will arise in many minds: why can't we just add this live foods program to our regular diet? For one very good reason. Your regular diet (if you are the average American) consists of dead food, and if you eat it long enough, you will be dead too—long before your time. If you want to live, and live healthily, you have to eat live food, and nothing but live food.

I remember many years ago when we had a television set (we don't any more, which has contributed greatly to our health and peace of mind) we used to watch Jackie Gleason in his "Honeymooners" program. His side kick, Art Carney, would be slumped over a counter at the local greasy spoon, and as Jackie came up from behind he would give him a resounding slap on the back and roar, "What's that slop you're eating?" Whereupon Art would ungracefully spit out the slop upon the counter. It was a very funny situation and never failed to get a laugh, from us at least.

But it is really tragic, not funny, for what Art Carney was no doubt eating makes up the customary diet of the average American family. And because of that diet, to a large extent, we guzzle "foodless foods" that aren't fit to feed the hogs, with the result we squander our hard earned money on doctors, drugs and hospitals — and still health eludes us.

Doctors, of course, can't be blamed for this sad state of affairs, for nutritional science forms an insignificant part of the medical curriculum. Hence they too are the victims of dietetic ignorance as much as their patients. They study sickness, not health.

By the way, did you ever notice that many doctors are as sick as the patients they treat? If you want to find out what disease you have, the doctors can tell you — correctly about 50% of the time, according to medical statistics. But if you want to find out about health you have to listen to those who have proved it in their own lives. Once again, the test of truth is: does it work? The live food program proves it does; the cooked food program proves it doesn't. It's that simple. You don't have to take our word for it. Try it, and prove to yourself the truth of what we say.

Man's Most Diabolical Enemy

One of the biggest hurdles you have to jump (so did we, just like everyone else on the live food regime) is to sentence to outer darkness the most mischief making organ in the body. You don't know what that is? I'll tell you. The TONGUE. All our lives we have given slavish obedience to its taste buds, and in so doing we have sold our health down the river of death. The tongue is the great god Moloch before whom we all bow down, worship, and to whom we sacrifice our birthright of health and life—for the mess of pottage composed of dead food, which rewards us with untold suffering, disease and premature death. For it's sad but true, most of what we eat we eat because it tastes good. But what tastes so good oftentimes is poison to our bodies, not nourishment.

In this category we find meat, most starches, potatoes, cereals, white flour, white sugar, candy, eggs, dairy products, pastries, salt, tea, coffee, tobacco, liquor and many other kindred items that taste good but are deadly to a human body. We have to train ourselves to eat to live, not live to eat.

The Law of Surplus Energy

Living to eat instead of eating to live leads to one of our besetting national sins: over-eating, which causes so much trouble in the digestive system. Witness the annual gluttony feasts of Thanksgiving and Christmas when the victims hastily hunt for the nearest bed or couch on which to "sleep it off." Ehret postulated a law, which our experience and that of others we know on the live food program, proves true: the more you eat the less energy; the less you eat the more energy, that is, when you eat raw food.

So if you are looking for a way out of the disease jungle in which we all are trapped, why not consider gradually giving up everything in your diet which is not actual nourishment. Feed your body that which it <u>needs,</u> not that which it <u>desires,</u> and you will be amazed at how little food you can live and thrive on. We hope this book will serve as an incentive for you to educate yourself in this new space age system of body feeding. You will find it will enrich your life and that of your family. Especially is this true in the case of young children. It will give them strong, healthy, disease-free bodies and save them years of agonizing effort to undo the follies of a foodless food regime.

Let's Live — and Live Abundantly

It seems incredible to us, but over and over again people ask us, "Where in the world do you get all these things you use?" Well, the best place we know is your local health food or specialty food store. If you don't happen to live in a city where such exist, subscribe to the best health magazines in the field of health.

In our home library the basic textbook is Prof. Arnold Ehret's great classic, "The Mucusless Diet Healing System." And it is just that, if followed faithfully. Ehret was a hundred years ahead of his time. Nutritionists are just now beginning to catch a faint glimmer of the brilliant light he shed on the problems of health and disease. More and more of them are espousing the principles he was one of the first, if not the first, to enunciate.

Dr. N. W. Walker's books on "Diet & Salad Suggestions" and "Raw Vegetable Juices"; Dr. H. E. Kirschner's "Live Food Juices"; Dr. John Richter's "Nature the Healer" and his wife Vera's "The Cookless Book"; J. I. Rodale's encyclopedic volume, "The Complete Book of Food & Nutrition," and his two magazines, "Organic Farming" and "Prevention" are all valuable additions to your library and will give you vast amounts of priceless health information you can get from no other source.

Most of these can be purchased from any health food store, along with the utensils and unusual products Doris uses in her kitchen, such as the food grinder, nut mill, juicer and blender. She says she couldn't live without her blender. You can, in fact, live almost entirely out of it if need be. But the other utensils have their place and add variety and spice to our meals.

To answer the question posed at the beginning of this book, Is Total Health Possible? —let me assure you that, based on our own experience in the last three years, you have it within your grasp if you but reach out for it —and stick with it. And without all the costly, time-consuming methods you have heretofore employed. You can unshackle yourself from the binding slavery to your stove. And you will save gobs of money in the process. Don't you think all this is worth the effort? We have found it so, and hope you will too.

Remember always that body health is but a means to an end, not the end itself. How often have we seen good, well meaning folks become so enamored with the idea of pursuing the goal of health, through live foods or any other means, that they unwittingly become fanatics, confusing the means with the end. Man is not an animal whose law of life requires it to spend most of its time searching for and consuming food. The true end of human life is mental and spiritual unfoldment. The body is but a horse to carry the real you to that destination. May we suggest, therefore, that you keep your eye on the goal, not the horse. Once you cleanse your body temple, forget about food. Take it as a natural course of events in your daily life, without constantly thinking and talking about it to anyone who will listen, and concentrate on the more worthwhile phases of life. A wise evangelist once said: "Spinach is no substitute for salvation." And one of the wisest men who ever lived told us that "Man shall not live by bread alone . . . ." Bread for the soul and spirit is equally as important as bread for the body.

We realize that many of you who read this book cannot or will not follow 100% the suggestions we make. For that reason we publish recipes that cannot be classed as completely pure raw food. As Prof. Ehret included in his book a transition diet, so do we feel that many of our suggestions come in the same category. We consider the highest and best diet for man is a strict fruit regime, as Ehret emphasized in his teachings. We have not reached that goal yet, but we are working towards it. We are about 90% along the way. Those who have reached, and maintained, the 100% level say they have acquired health, peace of mind and serenity of soul that are literally indescribable. Our experience thus far corroborates their testimony, and makes us confident that anyone can reach that goal if he will but try.

Slay the Adversary

In your quest for health, remember you battle an adversary (the false appetite for foodless foods) whose strength has been built up, in most cases, over a lifetime of habit, constantly fanned by the flames of desire, which often devours the best of intentions to eat live food and eliminate dead foods.

This is strikingly similar to the problem faced by the drug, the alcohol and the tobacco addict. Food oftentimes is as much of an escape mechanism as drugs, liquor and tobacco.

As in the case of members of Alcoholics Anonymous, who can remain sober only by calling on a power greater than themselves, exactly so for the dead food addict. Unless you have a superhuman will, which most people don't, and I certainly didn't, all your good intentions to stay on the live food program will go down the drain when the crises come, as come they will. In our own strength we are helpless to overcome that great and powerful adversary of the body — the TONGUE. Consider what the apostle James says about it in the Bible:

"And the tongue is a fire, a world of iniquity: so is the tongue among our members, that it defileth the whole body, and setteth on fire the course of nature . . . ."

His other references to the tongue relate to it as one member of the organ of speech, whereby we use it to bless and curse with words. But in this verse just quoted, especially the phrase, "it defileth the whole body," could it not just as well refer to the terrible temptation of its taste buds? Whether or not James actually had this thought in mind we can't say. But as a practical matter we know that it works this way in our everyday life.

Originally our taste buds in the tongue served the function of warning us what not to eat and also what was good for the body. But centuries of degeneration resulting from inherited false beliefs about nutrition have dulled its sensibilities so that as a body sentry it is now, in most people, sound asleep. Thus it allows the enemies of the body easy entry. After the cleansing of the body with live foods, it awakens and begins to perform its natural function of guarding the temple. You will experience taste sensations you never dreamed of before; you will enjoy your food in a way you never thought possible; and best of all, you will discover a bodily health you never knew could exist.

Prof. Ehret tells us of his outstanding exploits after two years of living on nothing but fruit. At the age of 31 he ran two and a quarter hours without a stop. At age 39, after a seven day fast, followed by only one meal of two lbs. of cherries, he made an endurance march through northern Italy of fifty-six hours without a stop, with no food, rest or sleep, only drink. Completing a sixteen hour walk he did 360 knee bends with arms extended. This by a man given up to die by his medical doctors.

Dr. Barbara Moore tells how she lived for three months in the mountains of Switzerland, eating nothing but snow and drinking only snow water. She climbed the mountains every day, often walking as far as sixty miles. She works constantly, with only two or three hours of sleep, never getting tired or hungry. Her two cross country walks from San Francisco to New York made her world famous.

Even more fantastic are the cases of the Bavarian stigmatist, Therese Neumann, and Giri Bala of India. Miss Neumann's case is, of course, world famous, and has been carefully verified many times. Going through the agony of the crucifixion every Friday, she has lived her entire adult life on nothing but one communion wafer once a day. Giri Bala's case is practically unknown, or was until it was first brought to the world's notice by Paramhansa Yogananda in his "Autobiography of a Yogi." Her amazing story has also been thoroughly verified. For fifty-five years she lived without eating! During all that time she prepared all the meals for her family, lived an active life, yet had no appetite for food. Both of these women maintain they live on God's light. When asked to explain, they say their secret cannot be revealed, that it is not for the mass of mankind, in this day, but only to prove that man is spirit, and that ultimately that spirit will rule the flesh.

In the Bible we have accounts of so-called miracles performed through fasting and prayer. Jesus is reported to have fasted forty days and nights when tempted on the mountain by the devil. And He tells us that those who believe on Him, greater works shall they do than He did.

Saints down through the ages have proven this promise of Jesus. Dr. Bucke in his monumental work on "Cosmic Consciousness" recounts the miraculous expansion of consciousness of outstanding men and women, as well as very ordinary and humble persons.

Many sincere people, stumbling in the darkness of modern secular education, are now trying to achieve this spiritual awareness in a mistaken belief in the powers of LSD and other soul, mind and body destroying psychedelic drugs. Yet the secret is simple, not complicated. All that is necessary is to cleanse the body temple, not poison it with deadly drugs. That secret is the live food regime, which, if followed faithfully, will eventually bring spiritual awareness and heightened powers.

Even in our own limited experience we have touched the outer fringes of that super-physical world the Masters of every age and time have demonstrated in their lives, and which Ehret hints at in his writings. And it can be done with complete safety, without flirting with the horrors produced by drugs.

But there is a price to pay, and it's a rather steep one, which very few feel they can afford. The coin we must present is the slain dragon of the tongue that guards the temple of light and life. And in battling that adversary we have found it of the utmost importance to call daily on divine aid in our warfare against the temptations of taste.

If you decide to go all out on the live food program, we sincerely urge you to do likewise, not only when the cleasing crises emerge, but as a daily routine. You will find, as we have, that that help is always available and invaluable. We all of us need that help—always, not only for controlling the tongue, but in every single one of life's problems.

The world looks to disarmament conferences, treaties, pacts, common market cartels, new inventions and every other imaginable kind of man-made panacea, none of which solve the world's problems. But you and I individually must look to the metaphysical Himalayan heights from whence cometh our strength.

If only the rulers of the world could do that, health, peace and prosperity would come to all.

There is only one true source of help. That is why the inspiring Spirit of our Scriptures says: "Without Me you can do nothing."

May the blessings of that Spirit be always with you.

GRAPEFRUIT DELIGHT

2 grapefruit
1 orange
12 sprigs of parsley

Juice grapefruit and orange. Put juice in blender. Add parsley and liquefy for 2 minutes or until parsley is well chopped. This makes a drink of cool mint green color. Can be served with crushed ice. Serve immediately.

CRANBERRY COCKTAIL

3 parts cranberry juice
1 part orange juice

Stir together. Serve with a thin slice of orange in each glass. Add crushed ice.

MINT TEA

1 or 1-1/2 teaspoons of peppermint tea to 1 cup of boiling water. Boil water, add tea and let steep from 5 to 10 minutes. Serve as an after dinner drink or between meals. Fresh ground mint can be used for this tea. Sweeten with honey.

COCONUT CREAM

Water from the inside of coconut
1 banana
2 cups of apricot nectar or pineapple juice
        Liquefy in blender until well blended.
Chill and serve. If desired, add more banana
to thicken.

COCONUT SUPREME

Water from the inside of coconut
2 cups of pineapple juice
2 cups of crushed pineapple
1 banana
1 cup of fresh grated coconut
        Liquefy coconut water, juice and fruit.
Pour into chilled glasses. Serve 1 spoonful of
grated coconut in each glass. If desired, add
more banana to thicken.

        Coconuts are rich in calcium, chlorine,
phosphorus, sulphur, sodium, magnesium, potassium and iron. They contain vitamins A, B
and G. Serve them often.

Many people seem to have an incurable "sweet tooth." If you are one of those and you want to satisfy it, but without the harm that comes from using white sugar, which is the base of so much sweetening, then we recommend you substitute carob. It has a delicious chocolate taste and children as well as grown-ups love it.

Carob is made from grinding the pulp in the pods of the carob tree which grows in the Holy Land and in the Mediterranean regions. The pods are fed to animals. They are mentioned in the Bible, where "he would fain have filled his belly with the husks the swine did eat." It formed the food which John the Baptist ate in the wilderness, hence sometimes called "St. John's Bread."

Carob has a fair amount of vitamins and minerals, but its chief virtue is as a chocolate substitute. Chocolate and cocoa, while rich in calcium, also contain considerable amounts of caffeine, theobromine and oxalic acid, stimulants the body can do without. The oxalic acid not only renders the calcium unavailable to the body, but also robs the body of its stored calcium. Many doctors feel chocolate is responsible in large measure for the adolescent problem of acne and forbid it to their patients. Like Sesame (or Tahini), Carob has a delicious flavor without the harmful qualities of chocolate. We highly recommend it as a substitute that all your family will enjoy. Carob can be purchased in health food or specialty food stores.

CAROB DRINK

2 tablespoons of almond nut butter
1 tablespoon of honey
4 teaspoons of carob flour
1 banana
3 cups of apricot juice or pineapple juice
    Liquefy in blender until well blended. Serve between meals.

CAROB CUP

3 cups of almond nut butter cream
(See recipe for almond cream, page 42.)
1 tablespoon of honey
4 teaspoons of carob flour
1 banana
    Liquefy until well blended. Serve as a breakfast drink.

CUP OF GOLD

Juice enough carrots in juicer machine to fill an 8 oz. glass per person. Serve about 20 minutes before meals or serve between meals.

VARIATIONS

Add 1/4 cup of celery juice to 1 cup of carrot juice
Add 1/4 cup of cucumber juice and 1/4 cup of celery juice to 1 cup of carrot juice.

Carrots are called king of the vegetable family and should be included in the diet in some form at least once a day.

VEGETABLE COCKTAIL

Put into blender: 3 cups of water or tomato juice, 2 tomatoes, 1 stalk of celery, 1 slice of green pepper, 1 green onion and 10 sprigs of parsley. Liquefy until well blended. If desired, season with broth powder, kelp or vegetable salt.

PEANUT BUTTER CREAM

Soak 1 cup of raisins in 2 cups of warm water for 2 hours. Drain water from raisins and put water in blender. Add 1 tablespoon of honey and 4 tablespoons of peanut butter. Liquefy until well blended. Serve on fruits or puddings. The soaked raisins can be served on chopped apples or puddings.

ALMOND NUT BUTTER CREAM

Almond nut butter can be substituted for peanut butter in the above recipe. This makes a delicious almond cream and can be used the same as peanut butter cream.

ALMOND NUT MILK

Use blanched or unblanched almonds. Soak nuts over night in apple juice or honey water. Use 1 cup of nuts to 2 cups of liquid. After the nuts are softened, put into blender and liquefy for about 2 minutes, or until nuts are finely chopped. Strain through sieve. Almond milk is high in protein and makes a good alkaline drink.

SESAME SEED MILK

1/2 cup of sesame seeds to 1-1/2 cups of water. Put seeds in blender and blend until seeds are well chopped. Add water and liquefy until well mixed. Honey, banana or carob can be added for flavor and nutrition. Liquefy until well blended. When the banana is added it is a wonderful drink for thin people to gain weight. The carob gives this drink a chocolate flavor.

SUNFLOWER SEED MILK

1 cup of sunflower seed
2 cups of water
Put seeds in blender and blend until seeds are well chopped. Add water and liquefy until well mixed. Honey can be added to sweeten. This is a good protein drink.

TAHINI

Sesame, from which Tahini is made, is one of the earliest seed crops cultivated by man. Products made from sesame have formed the basis of nutrition for many people. It makes an excellent substitute for eggs in making your own salad dressing and a fine substitute for milk for those allergic to milk. We recommend its use whenever possible.

Sesame seeds contain an amazing amount of calcium. According to the Agriculture Handbook No. 34 published by the United States Department of Agriculture, sesame seed has 1,125 milligrams of calcium for every 100 grams, about one-fourth pound. This is much higher than other calcium rich foods, such as soybeans, 227 milligrams; 590 milligrams in a pint of milk; 230 milligrams in a fourth pound of almonds; 1,086 milligrams for Swiss cheese. Cheese and milk, of course, are cooked products, which lowers their food value, while sesame is a live product. Whenever possible we should always eat live food in preference to cooked or dead food.

Sesame seeds contain high protein, from 19 to 28 per cent, more than many meats. Also lecithin, which helps to keep the fatty acids in the body low and in a fluid state. Also several of the B vitamins and E.

One of sesame's finest characteristics is its delicious taste. Sesame seeds and Tahini can be purchased in health food or specialty food stores. You will find it well worth your money.

———————

Health is God-given -- not something we buy in a bottle.

APPLES-RAISINS

2 apples
1 cup of raisins
2 cups of water
1/2 cup of sunflower seeds

Soak raisins and sunflower seeds in warm water for 1 hour. Grate apples in medium grader. Put apples in cereal bowls. Add 2 spoonfuls of soaked raisins and seeds over apples. Serve with peanut butter cream or almond nut butter cream. The juice from the soaked raisins can be used to make the nut butter cream.

APPLE BANANA

2 apples
1 cup of raisins
1 banana
2 cups of water

Soak raisins in warm water until soft. Drain raisins and put on top of chopped apples. Slice banana over apples and raisins. Serve with almond nut butter cream. The juice from the soaked raisins can be used to make the almond nut butter cream.

Watermelon or cantaloupe makes an excellent breakfast when in season.

Fresh coconut grated fine or date sugar sprinkled over fresh fruit makes a very nutritious breakfast.

Yogurt served on top of fresh fruit makes an excellent breakfast.

PRUNE WHIP

Soak 2 cups of dried prunes in enough prune juice or apple juice to cover. Let soak over night or until prunes are soft. Remove seeds and put prunes through a coarse sieve or put in blender and liquefy with just enough juice to make a thick sauce. Serve with fresh grated coconut or yogurt.

GRATED COCONUT

Cut fresh coconut in small pieces and put in nut mill. Grind until coconut is finely grated.

APPLE SAUCE

Cut apples in small pieces and put in blender. Liquefy, adding enough apple juice to make a medium sauce. Add honey to sweeten. Cinnamon, nutmeg, aniseeds or caraway seeds may be added for flavor.

———

The following are some of John Martin Reinecke's breakfast suggestions:

Winter
2 Delicious apples. 1 avocado. Handful of walnuts if desired. If still hungry, eat more.

2 pears. 1 avocado or handful of almonds or both. (Eat more or less, as desired.)

Spring
1 lb. of cherries. 1 avocado. Handful of pignolias if desired. (Substitute any other fruits.)

1 lb. of apricots. 1 avocado. Sunflower seeds. (Drink carrot-coconut juice any meal.)

Summer
1 lb. of peaches. 1 avocado. Handful of pecans. (Substitute raw almond butter for avocado.

All watermelon desired. Handful of sunflower seeds or nuts. (Substitute any other melon.)

Fall

Grapes or persimmons. 1 avocado. Filberts. Honey, coconut. (If desired, substitute soaked dried fruits.)

COCONUT-APPLE PORRIDGE

2 peeled-grated apples
3 walnuts
6 spoonfuls of coconut gratings
Juice of 1/2 lemon
Whole avocado
3 dates

Liquefy by adding little distilled water or 1 orange.

COCONUT CREAM MUSH

2 pears
1 orange
1/2 banana
3 pecan nuts
Comb honey

Liquefy. Top with coconut gratings. Any fruits in season you can substitute for pears. Flavor with bay leaf if desired. Any of these meals can be eaten as is without liquefying. Use juicy raw things abundantly.

AVOCADO SOUP

2 cups of water
2 cups of tomato juice
1 medium size carrot
2 stocks of celery
1 slice of onion or 1 green onion
2 tomatoes
1 avocado
Herbs, onion salt, vegetable salt or kelp to season.

Put water and tomato juice in blender. Cut vegetables in small pieces and add to liquid in blender. Liquefy until smooth. Add seasonings. Heat to not over 120 degrees F. Serve plain or with finely chopped parsley.

PEA SOUP

3 cups of water
1 package of frozen peas or 2 cups of fresh peas
1 green onion
1 large tomato
1 avocado
2 tablespoons of broth powder or
2 bouillon cubes
Vegetable salt or kelp to season

Heat to not over 120 degrees F. and serve.

BROTH SOUP

2 cups of water
2 cups of tomato juice
4 teaspoons of broth powder
12 sprigs of parsley

Heat water and tomato juice. Add broth powder. Sprinkle finely chopped parsley or soup garnishes on top of broth and serve. (See page 78 for RELISHES AND GARNISHES.)

TOMATO SOUP

3 cups of tomato juice
1 medium size tomato
1 medium size carrot
1 slice of onion
1 slice of green pepper
1/4 cup of almond nut butter
2 tablespoons of broth powder or
2 bouillon cubes

Put tomato juice in blender. Add chopped vegetables and nut butter. Liquefy until finely chopped. 1 avocado may be added to this soup. The avocado gives a thick smooth texture. Add seasonings and heat to not over 120 degrees F. Serve plain or with finely chopped parsley or soup garnishes. (See page 78.)

LIMA BEAN SOUP

1 package of frozen lima beans or 2 cups of
fresh beans
1 cup of water
2 cups of tomato juice
6 spinach leaves
10 sprigs of parsley
1 avocado

Liquefy vegetables with liquids in blender until smooth. Season with herbs and vegetable salt or kelp. Heat to low temperature,
not over 120 degrees F.

VEGETABLE SOUP

2 carrots
3 stalks of celery
1 package of frozen peas or 2 cups of fresh peas
1 package of frozen lima beans or 2 cups of fresh
lima beans
1 tomato
4 tablespoons of olive oil
6 cups of water or tomato juice

Grate carrots fine. Cut celery in small
pieces. Heat olive oil in pan. Add vegetables
and steam for 5 minutes on low heat. Add water
or tomato juice and reheat to low temperature.
Serve with grated parsley. Season with onion
salt, vegetable salt or kelp to taste.

CREAM OF CORN SOUP

2 cups of tomato juice
2 cups of water
1 package of frozen corn or 2 cups of fresh corn
1 green onion
1/4 cup of peanut butter or almond nut butter or
1 avocado

Season with herbs, broth powder and kelp. Fines herbs can be used. Liquefy in blender and heat to low temperature. Serve with finely chopped spinach leaves or parsley.

FRUIT SOUP

2 cups of orange juice
2 cups of pineapple juice
1/4 cup of almond nut butter
1 banana

Liquefy juice, nut butter and banana until creamy. Serve in bouillon bowls. Fresh sliced strawberries or other fresh berries can be added to bowl of soup. The added berries will make the soup attractive as well as nutritious.

VARIATIONS

Use your favorite fruit juice and fruit. This is very good with papaya, orange juice, banana and a few dates or raisins. Liquefy.

ONION SOUP

2 cups of chopped onions
4 cups of tomato juice
2 cups of water
1 cup of diced celery
2 tablespoons of broth powder
8 drops of soya sauce
10 sprigs of parsley

Liquefy in blender until onions, celery and parsley are coarsely chopped. Heat to low temperature and serve with grated parsley, or soup garnishes. (See page 78.)

CREAM OF ONION SOUP

2 cups of chopped onions
1 cup of chopped carrots
1 cup of diced celery
4 cups of tomato juice
2 cups of water
3 tablespoons of broth powder
2 tablespoons of soya sauce
1/4 cup of almond nut butter or avocado
10 sprigs of parsley

Liquefy in blender until smooth. Heat to not over 120 degrees F. Serve with soup garnishes. (See page 78.)

BORSCH
(Sour Cream)

2 cups of commercial sour cream or yogurt
2 cups of raw diced beets
1 green onion
     Put in blender and liquefy until well chopped. Season with kelp or vegetable salt. Serve cold, topped with sour cream or yogurt.

BORSCH
(Almond Nut Butter)

2 cups of raw diced beets
3 cups of water
1 green onion
1/2 cup of almond nut butter
1 tablespoon of broth powder
     Put ingredients in blender and liquefy until well chopped. Serve cold. Top with sour cream or yogurt.

VICHYSOISSE

     Grate enough potatoes to make 2 cups. Rinse off starch. Add 1 cup of boiling water and steam for 5 minutes on low heat. While potatoes are steaming, put in blender:
(continued)

3 cups of water
2 stalks of celery
1 green onion
3 teaspoons of broth powder
1 teaspoon of Fines herbs
1 avocado or 1/2 cup of almond nut butter

Add potato and water and blend together. Serve cold or warm. Serve with finely chopped parsley.

Fines herbs can be purchased in grocery stores.

Broth powder, kelp and bouillon cubes can be purchased in health food stores or specialty food stores. They take the place of salt for salt free diets.

KELP

How salt ever came to be such an important part of cooking is a great mystery. Perhaps, because cooking virtually destroys the value and natural taste of food, salt and other spices and condiments had to be added to make it somewhat palatable. Be that as it may, it is most harmful and should be eliminated as much and as soon as possible. On the live or raw food system you will find that after you become used to it you will never miss salt; in fact, you will be amazed how tasty your food becomes as you enjoy its natural flavors. Your taste buds will come alive again and give you taste thrills you never knew before.

For those of you who simply must have salt on your food, we recommend you substitute sea salt as a starter. It contains 75% of the very harmful drug sodium chloride, to which is often added potassium idodide. If you wish to boost your high blood pressure, contribute to overweight, hardening of the arteries and so on, use plenty of ordinary table salt, which contains 100% sodium chloride, a completely dead and very harmful substance.

A far better substitute we have found is kelp, which contains only about 18% sodium chloride, plus a high content of organic minerals and trace elements usable by the body. One of the finest elements in kelp is iodine, so helpful in controlling goiter. Kelp tastes delicious either taken alone or sprinkled on salads or vegetables. It can be purchased in health food or specialty food stores.

———————

Live foods are the best "medicine" for toxemia you can take.

TOSSED GREEN SALAD

Cut lettuce and endive in medium size pieces and put in salad bowl. Shred red cabbage and carrots and add to lettuce. Add chopped green onions. Serve with oil-lemon dressing.

VEGETABLE SALAD

Cut desired amount of cauliflower, celery, green onions and cucumber and put into a salad bowl of chopped lettuce. Add fresh or frozen peas or lima beans. Toss together and serve with tomato dressing or oil and lemon dressing.

BEAN SPROUT SALAD

Mix bean sprouts with diced Zucchini squash. Serve in salad bowls and top with wedges of tomato and avocado. Serve with tomato dressing. Shredded carrots can be added to this for variety and color.

CARROT-RAISIN-SALAD

Shred carrots fine. Add raisins and chopped pecans. Serve with mayonnaise or fruit dressing. Cubes of pineapple can be added for variety.

COLE SLAW # 1

Shred cabbage very fine. Add finely chopped onion. Serve with mayonnaise or tomato dressing.

COLE SLAW # 2

Shred cabbage very fine. Add small cubes of fresh pineapple. Serve with fruit dressing.

GREEN BEAN SALAD

Chop desired amount of green beans. Mix with finely chopped spinach leaves. Add small amount of green pepper and chopped green onion. Add diced celery. Mix together and serve on finely chopped lettuce leaf. Serve with tomato dressing.

LETTUCE SALAD

Cut medium size head of lettuce into wedges. Serve on salad plate. Top with tomato dressing in which diced onion, green pepper, celery and green beans have been added.

AVOCADO & TOMATO

Peel avocado and remove seed
Cut in medium size pieces
Add wedges of tomato
1 stalk of celery cut in small pieces
Toss together and serve on chopped lettuce. Serve with your favorite salad dressing.

CABBAGE SALAD

Equal parts of red and green cabbage
1 tomato
1 cup of chopped celery
1 small cucumber
1/2 teaspoon of Dill seeds
Mayonnaise
To 2 cups of chopped cabbage add 1 tomato cut in small pieces, 1 cup of finely chopped celery and 1 small cucumber cut in small pieces. Mix together. Add 1/2 teaspoon of Dill seeds and enough mayonnaise to moisten.

RAW POTATO SALAD

2 cups of medium grated potatoes
1 stalk of celery
1 green onion
1/2 lemon
1 teaspoon of celery seeds
1 cup of diced cucumber
1 teaspoon of Dill seeds
Kelp to season

Grate potato with medium size gricer. Rinse off starch. Add lemon juice and enough water to cover potato. Let soak for a few minutes. Drain off lemon water from potatoes. Add diced cucumbers, celery and green onion to the potatoes. Season with celery seeds, Dill seeds and kelp. Add mayonnaise or tomato salad dressing. Garnish with minced parsley and paprika.

WARM POTATO SALAD

2 cups of grated potato
1 stalk of celery
1 green onion
Slice of green pepper
Celery seeds and kelp to season

Grate potato with medium size gricer. Rinse of starch. Add small amount of water and steam for five minutes. Drain off water.
(continued)

Add vegetables and seasoning. Add mayonnaise or tomato salad dressing. Garnish with minced parsley.

BANANA PEANUT SALAD

1 cup of peanuts (unsalted)
3 bananas
1 stalk of celery

Chop peanuts medium size. Add sliced bananas and diced celery. Add just enough mayonnaise to moisten. Serve on chopped lettuce or lettuce leaf.

FRUIT SALAD

Put a layer of orange wedges and sliced bananas in salad bowl. Top with a few cubes of pineapple and prunes that have been stuffed with almond nut butter. Serve with fruit dressing.

SUMMER FRUIT SALAD # 1

Cut the heart from a head of lettuce. Press with palm of hand in order to separate the leaves so they will be cup shaped. Wash by

(continued)

running water through head of lettuce. Drain water and let stand a few minutes with open part of head down on paper towels. Separate the leaves in cup shape and place on salad plate. Fill with the following: Sliced strawberries, sliced peaches, sliced bananas, cubes of pineapple and grapes. Top with grated coconut and serve with your favorite fruit salad dressing.

SUMMER FRUIT SALAD # 2

Desired amounts of fresh peaches, fresh apricots and fresh pineapple. Use equal amount of fruit. Cut in bite size. Mix together and serve in large fruit bowl or individual fruit dishes.

FALL FRUIT SALAD

Desired amounts of fresh pears, fresh apples, bananas and pecans. Dice pears and apples in bite size. Add slices of bananas and chopped pecans. Serve with fruit dressing and prunes stuffed with almond nut butter.

As many of our recipes call for peanut or almond nut butter, we suggest you get the 1 gal. tins wholesale from the nut houses (no pun intended!) in the large cities.

BASIC BLENDER MAYONNAISE

1/2 cup of lemon juice
2 tablespoons of honey
2 tablespoons of Tahini
1/4 cup of olive oil or any cold pressed oil

Put lemon juice in blender. Add honey and Tahini. Liquefy while adding the oil very slowly. Use enough oil to make the mayonnaise as thick as you desire. Put in glass jar and store in refrigerator.

VARIATIONS

Add to basic mayonnaise: 1 green onion and 1 medium size tomato. Liquefy together. 1/2 cup of tomato catsup or 1/4 cup of tomato catsup and 1/4 cup of cocktail sauce can be substituted for the tomato.

AVOCADO DRESSING

Add avocado to basic mayonnaise and liquefy until well blended.

ROQUEFORT DRESSING

Add to basic blender mayonnaise: 2 oz. of crumbled blue cheese or Roquefort cheese. 1/2 cup of sour cream. Liquefy together. Put in glass jar and store in refrigerator.

FRUIT SALAD DRESSING # 1

1 cup of orange juice
1 tablespoon of Tahini
1 tablespoon of olive oil
1 teaspoon of honey
Stir together or liquefy. Serve over fruit salads.

FRUIT SALAD DRESSING # 2

1 cup of orange juice
1 tablespoon of almond nut butter
1 teaspoon of honey
2 tablespoons of olive oil
Stir together or liquefy in blender until smooth. Serve on fruit salad.

OIL AND LEMON JUICE DRESSING

Mix desired amounts of oil and lemon juice. Add small amount of honey. Fines herbs can be added for flavor. Serve on tossed salad.

MOCK SHRIMP LOUIE

Leaf of Chinese Cabbage (1 leaf per serving)
Finely chopped lettuce
Chopped green onion
Finely shredded carrot
Avocado
Tomato
Peanut butter
Tomato juice, lemon juice or yogurt

Mix peanut butter with the lemon juice, tomato juice or yogurt just enough to flavor and also to thin the peanut butter. Spread on cabbage leaf about 1/8 inch thick. Fill leaf with the chopped lettuce, onion and shredded carrot which have been tossed together. Garnish top with wedges of avocado and tomato. Serve with curry sauce. The shredded carrot gives the appearance and taste of shrimp when mixed with the lettuce and peanut butter. This combination of food is rich in vitamin A.

MOCK CRAB LOUIE

Make the same as mock shrimp louie, only substitute finely grated turnip in place of carrot.

SUGGESTIONS FOR SHREDDED VEGETABLES

Medium grate 1 Zucchini squash. Add finely grated carrot. Mix together. Serve with lemon and oil dressing. Sprinkle top with chili powder.

Finely grated turnip. Serve with lemon and oil dressing. Top with sweet chili powder.

Finely grated beets served with lemon and oil dressing.

MOCK SALMON LOAF

Grind desired amount of carrots through food grinder. To 2 cups of carrots add 2 large stalks of celery, ground. Add 1 tablespoon of Tahini and 3 tablespoons of peanut butter. Season with onion salt, vegetable salt and Fines herbs. Add 1/4 cup of sunflower seed meal. Stir together until mixed. Fill a custard cup with this mixture and press until it is well molded. Turn out on individual dinner plates or on a leaf of lettuce that has been placed on a dinner plate. Serve with curry sauce and
(continued)

garnish with a sprig of parsley. The sunflower seed meal can be made by putting the seeds in a nut mill and grind until fine. This makes a very attractive and nutritious food when served with a helping of grated turnips or grated beets.

MOCK TURKEY

Celery
Almonds or pecans
Onion
Avocado
Parsley
Sage

Grind 1 bunch of celery, 1 green onion and parsley through food grinder. Drain off juice. Use juice for soup. Put 1 cup of almonds or pecans in nut mill or blender and grind until fine. Mash avocado with a fork until well mashed. Add nuts, avocado and sage to celery mixture. Shape in patties with a spoon and serve on a lettuce leaf. Serve with cranberry sauce.

CASHEW ALMOND LOAF

1 cup of cashews coarsely ground
1 cup of almonds coarsley ground
1 cup of ground coconut

(continued)

6 spinach leaves
12 sprigs of parsley
1 cup of diced carrots
1/2 cup of raisins

Put all ingredients through food grinder, except avocado. Mash avocado and mix with ingredients. Form into loaf.

CARROT SOUFFLE

2 cups of diced carrots
1 cup of diced apples
1 cup of apple juice
Blend together
1 tablespoon of Gelatin

Dissolve Gelatin in cold water. Mix with 1/4 cup of hot water. Add to other ingredients. Chill. Serve on lettuce leaf.

STUFFED CABBAGE ROLLS

1/2 cup of nuts (pecans or almonds) coarsely ground
1/2 cup of raisins or currants
1/4 cup of minced parsley
1 cup of diced apples

Mix together. Fill cabbage leaves and fasten with toothpicks.

PEAS AND CARROT CROQUETTES

1 package of frozen peas or 2 cups of fresh peas
2 cups of diced raw carrots
1 green onion
1/2 cup of sunflower seeds
2 teaspoons of kelp

Put peas, carrots, onion and sunflower seeds through food grinder. Mix together and add kelp. Form into patties and serve with curry sauce or mayonnaise. Finely grated parsley can be added for variety.

PEA CROQUETTES

1 package of frozen peas or 2 cups of fresh peas
6 leaves of spinach
1 stalk of celery
1 slice of green pepper
1 carrot (medium size)
1/4 cup of almond nut butter

Enough water or tomato juice in blender to blend vegetables. Blend vegetables, but not too fine. Pour into mixing bowl and add almond nut butter and 1 tablespoon of mayonnaise. This mixture should not be too thin. If too thin, add sunflower seed meal or ground nuts. Dip with ice cream dipper to shape like croquettes and place on individual dinner plates or on lettuce leaves. Garnish with parsley.

AVOCADO CROQUETTES

2 avocados
1 green onion
1 package of frozen lima beans or 2 cups of fresh lima beans
1 tablespoon of mayonnaise
1 teaspoon of broth powder, kelp or vegetable salt

Put in blender and liquefy until smooth. Dip with ice cream dipper to shape like croquettes. Serve on lettuce leaves.

STUFFED TOMATO

Scoop the pulp from the inside of tomatoes. Drain off juice. Put pulp in bowl. Add mayonnaise, minced parsley and ground pecans or sunflower seed meal to pulp. Mix together and fill tomatoes. You can use the tomato juice for soup. Garnish with a sprig of parsley.

STUFFED AVOCADO

Peel desired amount of avocados. Cut in half and remove seed. Fill with the following: Finely diced green beans, diced celery, chopped onion, fresh cauliflower buds cut in small pieces and a small amount of mayonnaise. Mix together and fill avocado halves.

STUFFED GREEN PEPPER

Use small green bell peppers. Cut off top and scoop out seeds. Fill with the following: Finely chopped cabbage, green onion, finely chopped parsley, Dill seed and mayonnaise. Mix together and fill bell peppers.

MEXICAN GUACAMOLE

3 avocados
Juice of 1/2 lemon
2 green onions
Mash avocados, add lemon juice and finely chopped onion.
Make tomato sauce as follows:
3 tomatoes
2 green onions
1 teaspoon of honey
1 teaspoon of lemon juice
1 tablespoon of olive oil
1 teaspoon of chili powder
Dash of cayenne pepper
Put all ingredients in blender and blend slightly.
Chop lettuce and put on individual dinner plates. Put the avocado mixture on the lettuce and top with the tomato sauce.

GOMA AE

3 cups of diced fresh green beans
1/4 cup of sesame seeds
2 fresh tomatoes, cut in small pieces
        Mix together and serve on plate. Top with avocado dip.

SUCCOTASH

1 package of frozen corn or 2 cups of fresh corn cut from cob
1 package of frozen lima beans or 2 cups of fresh lima beans
1 green onion
2 stalks of celery
1 tomato
1 teaspoon of curry powder
1 tablespoon of broth powder
        Cut green onion, celery and tomato in small pieces. Add to corn and beans. Add seasoning and heat to not over 120 degrees F.

OKRA

1 package of frozen okra or 2 cups of fresh okra
1 green onion
2 medium size tomatoes
1 stalk of celery
                (continued)

Cut onion, tomatoes and celery in small pieces and add to okra. Season with kelp or vegetable salt. Heat to low temperature and serve plain or topped with minced parsley.

CHICKEN A LA CHERYL

2 cups of chopped cauliflower. Use buds and parts of stems and leaves.
1 green onion
1 cup of chopped celery
1 teaspoon of Tahini
2 teaspoons of kelp
1/4 cup of almond nut butter
3 teaspoons of Instant Broth Powder (chicken style) or
3 chicken bouillon cubes

Grind onion, celery and cauliflower in food grinder. Add Tahini, kelp and Broth Powder to almond nut butter. Add to cauliflower. Mix together. Form into croquettes. Roll them slightly in wheat germ. Serve with curry sauce.

BROCCOLI PATTIES

2 cups of chopped broccoli
1 green onion
1/4 cup of peanut butter (raw, unsalted)

(continued)

3 teaspoons of kelp
1 teaspoon of Salvita or Vegex
1/2 teaspoon of Sage

Chop onion and broccoli fine, using both flower and stem of broccoli. Put through food grinder. Add all other ingredients. Mix together well. Form into patties and serve with tomato or chili sauce.

SUCCOTASH A LA KOOBATIAN

4 cups of frozen or fresh corn
2 avocados
2 tomatoes

Blend corn in blender with just enough water to liquefy. Remove from blender and add mashed avocados and small cubes of tomatoes. Season with broth powder and kelp. Heat to not over 120 degrees F.

MOCK TUNA FISH

2 cups of chopped parsnips
10 sprigs of parsley
1 slice of green pepper
1/4 cup of almond nut butter
3 tablespoons of mayonnaise
1 teaspoon of kelp

(continued)

Put parsnips, parsley and green pepper through food grinder. Add other ingredients and mix well. Form into patties or loaves and serve with tartar sauce.

FATHMANBURGER

1 cup of soaked lentils
1 cup of frozen or fresh corn
1 green onion
1/4 cup of peanut butter (raw, unsalted)
1 cup of chopped celery
1 teaspoon of Vegex or Salvita
2 teaspoons of Bacon Yeast
2 teaspoons of kelp

Soak lentils in warm water for four hours or overnight. Put soaked lentils, corn, onion and celery through food grinder. Add other ingredients and mix together. Form into patties. Serve with tomato sauce.

PARSNIP AND CARROT LOAF

2 cups of sliced parsnips
1 cup of sliced carrots
12 sprigs of parsley
1/4 cup of almond nut butter
1 teaspoon of broth powder
3 teaspoons of kelp

(continued)

Put parsnips, carrots and parsley through food grinder. Add other ingredients. Press in custard cup to form loaf. Turn out on lettuce leaves or individual dinner plates. Serve with tomato or curry sauce.

CABBAGE A LA KELI

Romaine lettuce (1 leaf per person)
Cabbage
Peanut butter
Mayonnaise
Peas
Tomatoes
Avocado

Spread peanut butter on romaine lettuce leaf. Grind desired amount of cabbage. Mix with a small amount of mayonnaise. Spread over peanut butter on lettuce leaf. Top with raw peas, wedges of tomatoes and avocado.

KELIBURGERS

2 cups of ground cabbage
2 avocados
1/2 cup of ground sunflower seeds
3 teaspoons of broth powder
1 cup of ground pecans

Grind enough cabbage through food grinder to make 2 cups full. Mash avocados and add
(continued)

to ground cabbage. Add broth powder and mix thoroughly. Form into patties and roll in ground pecans. Garnish with parsley and wedges of tomatoes.

RAW VEGETABLE-NUT LOAF
(Reinecke recipe)

One cup each of carrots and tomatoes which have been put through a food chopper, using the fine cutter. One cup of finely chopped or grated celery, 1/2 cup minced parsley, 1/2 cup of minced bell pepper, 2 tablespoons of oil and 1 clove of garlic which has been minced very finely and crushed. Now add a sufficient amount of ground raw peanuts or pignolias so that the mixture will be stiff enough to mould, mixing all ingredients well together. Place in oblong loaf pan which has been moistened slightly with cold-pressed oil. Place the loaf on a platter and garnish with parsley and green onions. Raw peanut butter dressing goes well with this. Many variations of flavor are possible with this vegetable-nut loaf by substituting sage or thyme, savory, dill, etc., for the parsley. Pistachio nuts substituted for the peanuts or the pignolias give an entirely different flavor. Garnish with parsley.

RELISH TRAY

Cauliflower buds
Carrot curls
Radish roses
Turnip sticks
Carrot sticks
Stuffed celery
Green onions
Celery hearts
Cherry tomatoes
Tomato slices
Bell peppers (sliced)

Use a combination of any of these vegetables and place on tray or platter in attractive arrangement.

Separate cauliflower into buds and wash. Sprinkle with Paprika or chili powder.

Carrot curls: slice very thin lengthwise and place in ice water to curl.

Radish roses. Cut top of radishes in shape of rose petals.

Turnip and carrot sticks. Cut in small thin sticks lengthwise. Serve plain or spread with avocado and lemon juice mixture.

Stuffed celery: stuff with a mixture of peanut butter and tomato juice, or peanut butter and lemon juice, or peanut butter and mayonnaise, or avocado and lemon juice.

(continued)

Green onions, celery hearts, cherry tomatoes and sliced tomatoes. Arrange on plate or tray with other relishes.

Green bell peppers. Cut in circles and arrange with other relishes, especially tomatoes. They are very colorful together.

For a buffet dinner, a tray of stuffed tomatoes, stuffed green bell peppers and stuffed avocados can be arranged among the other vegetables suggested for the relish tray.

FRUIT DISH

A compote dish or large platter filled with fresh fruit makes a very good lunch. Some suggested fruits for this combination are:

Small watermelon slices
Small cantaloupe slices
Apple slices with peanut butter and date spread
Banana slices dipped in mayonnaise and rolled in a mixture of coconut and ground nuts
Fresh strawberries
Orange slices
Stuffed dates with almond nut butter
Stuffed prunes with almond nut butter
Fresh cherries
Grapes

(continued)

Arrange any of these fruits on large platter. Decorate with a few sprigs of parsley. This makes a very attractive dish.

SOUP GARNISHES

Sesame seeds
Sunflower seeds
Sprouts
Grated or slivered nuts
Minced parsley, celery leaves, chives and mint leaves
Thin slices of carrots, turnips and cucumbers.

DRIED FRUITS

Dried apples, pears, apricots, peaches and prunes. These fruits can be purchased at health food or specialty food stores. Those purchased at supermarkets are dried with sulfur. Read contents on package first before you buy. Dried fruits are good for winter use or in recipes where you do not want juicy fruits. However, they should be soaked overnight to restore their moisture content, as this enhances their digestibility. _____

We dig our graves (prematurely) with our teeth. Don't be a grave digger -- by eating dead foods. Eat live foods and stay alive longer.

CURRY SAUCE

4 tablespoons of soy powder
1 teaspoon of curry powder
1/4 teaspoon of broth powder
Enough tomato juice or water to make a medium or thin sauce

Add liquid to soy powder and seasonings. If a thick sauce is desired, use less liquid. This is good to serve on mock salmon loaf or mock crab louie. 1 teaspoon of mayonnaise can be added to this if desired.

CRANBERRY SAUCE

Put in blender desired amount of cranberries, honey to sweeten and enough orange juice to blend the cranberries. This should be a thick sauce. It is very good to serve with the mock turkey at Christmas time.

A mucus-filled blood stream is like a stove pipe clogged with soot that has never been cleaned out. In reality, it's worse, because protein and starch waste makes it sticky.

AVOCADO DIP

2 avocados
1 tomato
1 finely minced green onion
1 tablespoon of basic mayonnaise
1 teaspoon Fines herbs
2 tablespoons of lemon juice
Dash of garlic powder

Mash avocados and tomatoes together. Add other ingredients. This can be used on the Goma Ae. (See recipe on page 72.) This dip can also be used to dip slices of cucumber and celery sticks.

TARTAR SAUCE

1 cup of basic mayonnaise
4 tablespoons of lemon juice
1/2 cup of diced cucumber (cut fine)
1 slice of finely chopped onion
1/8 cup of minced parsley

Mix together. Serve on mock salmon loaf or crab louie.

APPLE SAUCE

See recipe for "Suggestions for Breakfast."

STRAWBERRY SAUCE

Mash fresh or frozen strawberries. Add honey to sweeten. If too thin, add a little almond nut butter. Serve over ice cream or sherberts. Makes a very good strawberry sundae.

CAROB SAUCE
(Substitute for chocolate)

1/2 cup of soy powder
2 teaspoons of carob powder
3 tablespoons of honey
1/2 cup of water

Mix carob powder and honey to soy flour. Add water and stir until well mixed. Serve over ice cream. (See page 121.) Makes a very good fudge sundae. Top with grated coconut or chopped pecans. Use more or less water, depending on the desired thickness.

POPPY SEED SAUCE

4 tablespoons of soy flour
3 tablespoons of lemon or lime juice
2 tablespoons of poppy seeds
1 teaspoon of honey

Mix ingredients, using enough water to make a paste. Serve on vegetable loaf.

BUTTERSCOTCH SAUCE

18 pitted dates
1/2 cup of fig juice
Liquefy in blender until smooth. Serve over ice cream or sherberts. Makes a good butterscotch sundae.

BUTTERSCOTCH COCONUT SAUCE

12 pitted dates
1/2 cup of fig juice
1/2 cup of grated coconut
Liquefy dates and juice in blender until smooth. Pour into bowl and add coconut. Mix well. Serve over ice cream or sherbert.

TOMATO AND PEA DIP

1 package of frozen peas or 2 cups of fresh peas
2 tomatoes
8 drops of soya sauce
1 green onion
Garlic salt or 1/4 clove of fresh garlic
Kelp and broth powder to season
Liquefy together. This is a very good dip for celery sticks or cucumber slices. If too thick, add more tomato.

CAROB AND DATE SAUCE

12 dates
1 tablespoon of honey
1 teaspoon of carob flour

Remove pits from dates. Add honey, carob flour and enough water or fruit juice to make a paste. Mash with a fork to smooth consistency. Add more water to make the desired thickness of sauce. Good for ice cream topping.

CINNAMON SAUCE

1/2 cup of soy flour
3 tablespoons of honey
1 teaspoon of cinnamon
1/8 teaspoon of nutmeg
Water

Mix ingredients together, using enough water to make a medium sauce. Serve on mince pie.

SOY YOGURT

1/2 or 3/4 cups of soy flour to 1 quart of water
1 cup of yogurt starter

Make same as milk yogurt. Scald soy milk, then cool to luke warm. Add starter and let set in yogurt maker until jelled.

SOY COTTAGE CHEESE

2 cups of soy flour

Add enough cold water to make a paste. Add 1 quart of boiling water. Set on burner, using low heat or put in double boiler. Stir to keep from sticking or burning. Bring to a boil and simmer for 5 minutes. Remove from burner and add 1/2 cup of apple cider vinegar or lemon juice. Let stand for 5 minutes. Strain through fine sieve or cheese cloth. Use to make cheese cake or serve with chopped onions, kelp, garlic, chopped chives or parsley.

PEANUT BUTTER

Use raw, unsalted peanuts. Put small amount of peanuts in blender. Chop fine. Add enough peanut oil to liquefy to a peanut butter consistency.

TOMATO SAUCE

1/2 cup of soy powder
1 teaspoon of kelp
1 teaspoon of broth powder
1/4 cup of tomato catsup or tomato juice
Water

Mix together with small amount of water to make a thin paste. Serve on mock crab and shrimp louie.

COCONUT WHIPPED CREAM
(Substitute for whipped cream)

Use fresh coconut. Cut off brown peeling so the coconut cream will be white. Cut in small pieces, put in nut mill and grind until it is fine. Put in blender and add 4 tablespoons of almond nut butter to 2 cups of coconut. Add enough coconut water or plain water to liquefy. Add honey to sweeten and 1 teaspoon of vanilla. Liquefy until smooth like whipped cream. Serve on fresh fruit or ice cream. Dry coconut can be used, but less honey will be needed.

PAPAYA SAUCE

Peel papaya and remove seeds. Cut papaya in cubes and put in blender. Liquefy. To 2 cups of papaya add juice of one lemon. If this is too tart, a little honey can be added. Put in glass jar and store in refrigerator. This will jell overnight or in a few hours. Eat plain or serve with a dinner.

Mucus in the blood stream lowers the vital force of the body. This creates friction, like in a dirty engine or driving your car with the brakes on. Fruits loosen this mucus, creating a fever, like steam cleaning that dirty car engine.

JAMS AND BUTTERS

DATE BUTTER

20 dates
Prune juice

Remove pits from dates and put dates in blender. Add enough prune juice to liquefy to make a thick butter. Liquefy until smooth. Serve on apple slices or imitation rye bread.

DATE NUT BUTTER

Make same as date butter. Add 1 tablespoon of almond nut butter.

STRAWBERRY JAM

Use frozen or fresh strawberries. Put in blender and liquefy or mash with fork until berries are medium size pieces. Pour into bowl. Mix enough almond nut butter to make a thick jam. Sweeten with honey. Serve on apple slices or raw breads.

APRICOT JAM

Use fresh or frozen apricots. Put in blender. Add honey to sweeten. Mix almond nut butter to make a thick jam. Liquefy until smooth or mash with fork until blended together.

APRICOT BUTTER

Make the same as apricot jam, only add cinnamon and nutmeg to taste.

FIG BUTTER

Remove pits from 10 dates and put dates in blender. Add 10 figs and enough fig juice to liquefy to make a thick butter. Serve on apple slices or imitation rye bread.

CACTUS CUBES

Remove the ripe pears from the prickly pear cactus. Use a long 2 pointed fork to remove the pears. Wash off sharp stickers by a heavy force of water. Drain. Put in blender, a few at a time. Add enough apple juice to liquefy. Strain through a sieve. Pour into ice cube

(continued)

trays and freeze. When frozen, remove from trays, put cubes in a plastic bag and tie the top. Store in freezer until ready for use. These cubes can be used for making cold drinks, sherberts and puddings.

APRICOT CUBES

Use frozen or fresh apricots. Put apricots in blender. Add enough apple juice to liquefy. Pour into ice cube trays and freeze. When frozen, remove from trays and put cubes in a plastic bag and tie top. Store in freezer until ready for use. These cubes can be used for making cold drinks, sherberts and puddings.

DATES

In using dates for pie crusts and confections it is important to get the best type of date. Our experience seems to indicate the Khadrawi is ideal for this purpose because of its softness and high sugar content. Another important factor is to endeavor to get dates organically raised (usually available in health food and specialty food stores). Those you get in the ordinary markets have been gassed and sulphured and are not nearly as suitable as those organically raised.

IMITATION RYE

Grind equal parts of black mission figs and nuts. Use almonds, peanuts or pecans or a combination of these nuts. Add enough wheat germ to make stiff. Put all of this mixture through the food grinder again. This mixes it more thoroughly and is an important step. Form into a long roll or loaf. Wrap in wax paper. Keep in refrigerator. Slice thin when served.

CAROB RYE

Use the recipe for imitation rye and add 3 teaspoons of carob flour. Form into loaf, wrap in wax paper and keep in refrigerator until ready for use. Slice thin.

CORNMEAL AND RAISIN BREAD

1 cup of cornmeal
1/2 cup of soy flour
2 teaspoons of kelp
1/2 cup of almond nut butter
4 tablespoons of olive oil
1/4 cup of raisins
1/8 cup of water

(continued)

Put raisins through food grinder. Mix the cornmeal, soy flour, kelp, honey, almond nut butter and oil. Add to raisins. Mix together. Add water and form into a loaf. Wrap in wax paper and store in refrigerator.

CORNBREAD # 1

2 cups of cornmeal
1/2 cup of soy flour
1/2 cup of almond nut butter
4 tablespoons of olive oil
3 teaspoons of kelp
1 tablespoon of honey
1/2 cup of water.

Mix together, using just enough water to form into a loaf. Wrap in wax paper and store in refrigerator. Slice thin when ready to serve.

CORNBREAD # 2

2 cups of cornmeal
1 cup of soy flour
1/3 cup of finely ground cashew nuts
1/3 cup of finely ground sunflower seeds
1/3 cup of finely ground sesame seeds
2 teaspoons of kelp
4 tablespoons of honey
4 tablespoons of olive oil
1/4 cup of almond nut butter
(continued)

Mix dry ingredients. Add honey and oil. Mix together. Knead in nut butter. Add just enough water to make a dough. Add chopped dates if desired. Form into loaf. Wrap in wax paper and store in refrigerator. Slice thin and serve with date or fig butter.

NUT OATMEAL BREAD

1/3 cup of pecans
1/3 cup of almonds
1/3 cup of peanuts (unsalted)
1 cup of oatmeal
1/4 cup of soy flour
4 tablespoons of olive oil
2 teaspoons of kelp
1/2 cup of peanut butter
6 dates
1/4 cup of raisins

Grind nuts fine. Put raisins through food grinder. Mix ingredients together, except the water. Put through the food grinder again. Add water and form into loaf. Wrap in wax paper and store in refrigerator. Slice thin when ready to serve. This is good with any of the jams and butters. (See recipes on page 88.)

You're not tired -- just toxic. Flush the toxins out of your blood stream and you will drain away that tired from your body.

PEANUT BUTTER CRUST

1/2 cup of finely ground seeds. Use a mixture of alfalfa seed, sesame seed, flax seed and sunflower seed -- or in place of the seeds, use 1/2 cup of ground coconut
1/4 cup of finely ground peanuts (unsalted)
1/4 cup of peanut butter
3 teaspoons of kelp
3 tablespoons of honey
1/4 cup of soy flour
1 cup of oatmeal
4 tablespoons of water
4 tablespoons of olive oil

Mix dry ingredients. Knead in the peanut butter and honey. Put this mixture through the food grinder. This mixes it together and is an important step. Add the water to make a dough. Roll out on wax paper. Use soy flour to keep from sticking. Roll dough over a rolling pin and place over a pyrex pie plate. Unroll the dough off the rolling pin into the plate and shape into place. Fill with your choice of filling. This crust is good for mince pies and apple pies. Double the recipes so you will have enough for the top crust. Serve with cinnamon sauce. Use small portions because this is a rich pie.

CAROB NUT PIE CRUST

Use the recipe for peanut butter crust. Substitute almond nut butter for peanut butter. Add 4 teaspoons of carob flour to the dry ingredients. Prepare the same as peanut butter pie crust. Fill with your favorite filling. Carob filling or pecan filling is good for this crust. Any of these pie crusts can be stored in the refrigerator until ready for the filling.

DATE PIE CRUST

1 cup of oatmeal
1/2 cup of soy flour
2 teaspoons of kelp
1/4 cup of coconut
4 tablespoons of olive oil
1/4 cup of dates (12 dates)
3 tablespoons of water

Mix dry ingredients together. Add olive oil and the dates that have been ground through a food grinder. Knead until well mixed. Add water and knead into a dough. Roll out on wax paper, using soy flour to keep from sticking. Roll dough over rolling pin, place over pie plate and unroll dough into the pie plate. Shape into form and fill with your choice of filling.

DATE-CAROB CRUST

Use recipe for date pie crust. Add 3 teaspoons of carob flour to the dry ingredients. Prepare the same as date crust.

OATMEAL PIE CRUST

1 cup of oatmeal
1/2 cup of soy flour
1/4 cup of sesame seeds, ground fine
1/2 cup of wheat germ
1/4 cup of honey
4 tablespoons of olive oil or cooking oil
Few drops of water
Mix together, adding enough water to make a dough. Press in pie plate. Fill with pecan pie filling or your favorite pie filling.

OATMEAL-DATE PIE CRUST

2 cups of oatmeal
1/2 cup of soy flour
3 teaspoons of kelp
1/2 cup of wheat germ
1 cup of dates
4 tablespoons of olive oil
Mix oatmeal, soy flour, kelp and oil together. Knead in chopped dates. Add just enough water to make a stiff dough. Roll out and put in pie plate or put in pie plate and form into shape.

CAROB PIE CRUST
(Substitute for chocolate)

1-1/8 cups of finely ground seeds. (Use alfalfa, sesame, sunflower and flax seeds.)
1 teaspoon of cinnamon
1/2 teaspoon of nutmeg
5 teaspoons of carob
2 teaspoons of peanut butter
1/2 cup of dates (put through food grinder)
2 tablespoons of hard crystallized honey

Mix together. Add enough water to make a dough. To make a double pie crust, double the recipe and take out 1/2 of mixture for top of pie. Roll out on wax paper, using enough soy flour to keep from sticking, or this can be pressed and formed into the pie dish.

TARTS

Tarts can be made of these pie crusts instead of large pies. Press dough in small tart pans and fill with your favorite filling.

Ehret tells us that it requires from one to three years of the cleansing live food regime before the body rids itself of accumulated poisons -- depending on the age of the person and how much cooked or dead food he has eaten.

IMITATION CHOCOLATE CREAM PIE

3 cups of prune juice
1/2 cup of soy flour
5 teaspoons of carob flour
1/4 cup of honey
2 teaspoons of kelp
1 teaspoon of vanilla
1/4 cup of almond nut butter
2 tablespoons of vegetable Gelatin

Put all ingredients in blender except the Gelatin. Liquefy. Dissolve the Gelatin in 1/4 cup of cold water. When it is jelled, add hot water and dissolve. Add to the mixture in the blender. Liquefy together. Chill in blender bowl. When it is solid, liquefy again and pour into crust. This makes it creamy. 1/2 cup of Agar-Agar can be used in place of Gelatin. See directions on package and see article on Agar-Agar on page 104.

The tongue is not only the body's great adversary, but at the same time a "magic mirror." For it reflects the condition of not only the stomach but the entire membrane system as well. Live foods will keep this mirror clean.

BUTTERSCOTCH PIE

3 cups of fig juice
1/2 cup of soy flour
1/4 cup of almond nut butter
2 teaspoons of kelp
1 teaspoon of vanilla
1/4 cup of honey
2 tablespoons of vegetable Gelatin

    Liquefy all the ingredients in blender, except the Gelatin. Dissolve the Gelatin in cold water. When it is jelled, add hot water and dissolve. Add to the mixture in blender and liquefy. Chill until solid. Liquefy again and pour into crust. 1/2 cup of Agar-Agar can be used in place of Gelatin. See directions on package and see article on Agar-Agar on page 104.

BLUEBERRY PIE

3 cups of frozen or fresh blueberries
1/3 cup of honey
1 tablespoon of vegetable Gelatin

    Add honey to berries. Dissolve the Gelatin in 1/4 cup of cold water. When jelled, add 1/4 cup of hot water and dissolve. Add to the berries and mix together. Pour into pie crust and chill until solid.

LEMON PIE

2-1/2 cups of apple juice
1/4 cup of honey
1/2 cup of lemon juice
3 tablespoons of vegetable Gelatin

Mix apple juice, honey and lemon juice together. Dissolve Gelatin in 1/4 cup of cold water. When jelled, add hot water to dissolve. Add to lemon mixture. Beat well or liquefy. Pour into crust and chill.

LEMON CREAM PIE

2-1/2 cups of apple juice
1/4 cup of honey
1/2 cup of lemon juice
1/4 cup of almond nut butter
3 tablespoons of vegetable Gelatin

Mix all ingredients in blender, except the Gelatin. Dissolve Gelatin in 1/4 cup of cold water. When jelled, add hot water to dissolve. Add to mixture in blender and liquefy. Chill, and liquefy again when it is solid. This makes it creamy. Pour into crust and chill.

Vitality does not depend nearly so much on how much or what kind of food we eat as it does on how clean we keep the blood stream.

MINCE PIE

1 cup of raisins
1/2 cup of currants
6 dates
4 cups of apples
1 teaspoon of cinnamon
1/2 teaspoon of nutmeg
1 tablespoon of lemon juice

Grate apples through medium grater. Add lemon juice, spices and currants. Put dates and raisins through food grinder. Add to the apple mixture and mix together. Fill pie crust and cover with a thin crust. Use a fork to press the edges together. Serve with cinnamon sauce.

IMITATION PUMPKIN PIE

3 cups of finely grated sweet potatoes or yams
1 tablespoon of lemon juice
3 tablespoons of honey
1 teaspoon of cinnamon
1/4 teaspoon of nutmeg
1/2 cup of almond butter
12 dates
1/4 cup of soy flour

Grate sweet potatoes or yams through fine gricer. Add other ingredients and mix together. Fill pie crust and serve plain or with grated coconut.

APPLE PIE

4 cups of grated apples
⅓ cup of honey
1 teaspoon of cinnamon
½ teaspoon of nutmeg
1 tablespoon of lemon juice
¼ cup of almond nut butter

Grate apples through medium gricer. Add other ingredients. Fill pie crust and top with a thin crust or serve open face.

PECAN PIE

¾ cup shelled pecan nuts
1 cup of pitted dates
¼ cup of almond nut butter
½ cup of coarsely chopped almonds
1 cup of water
¼ cup of fig or prune juice
1 teaspoon of vanilla
½ cup of soy flour

Soften the dates in warm water. Mash with fork. Add vanilla and soy flour. Add water gradually until mixture is the right consistency to make a thick filling. Add nuts and fill pie crust. This is a very rich pie, so serve small portions. Use the carob nut pie crust or the oatmeal pie crust for this filling.

PEACH PIE

1 cup of peach juice
3 cups of frozen or fresh peaches
3 teaspoons of Agar-Agar
    If spicy peach pie is desired, add:
1 teaspoon of cinnamon
1/4 teaspoon of allspice
    Dissolve Agar-Agar according to directions on package. Also see article on Agar-Agar on page 104. Add to juice in blender and blend together. Add to other ingredients and fill pie crust. Let cool until jelled.

FRESH PEACH PIE
(9 inch pie crust)

4 cups of fresh peaches
3 teaspoons of Agar-Agar
1/4 cup of apple juice plus 1 medium size peach
3 or 4 dates or honey to sweeten
Spices may be added if spicy pie is desired
1 teaspoon of cinnamon
1/4 teaspoon of allspice or nutmeg
    Dissolve Agar-Agar according to directions. Also see article on Agar-Agar on page 104. Add Agar-Agar to juice in blender. Blend together. Add to other ingredients. Fill pie crust. Chill until jelled.

AGAR-AGAR & VEGETABLE GELATIN

We have included these items in some of our recipes for the purpose of providing a non-injurious thickening. Not much of it is needed. A little goes a long way. We urge you to use these <u>vegetable</u> products in preference to the ordinary animal products you get in the supermarket. Perhaps if we quote the dictionary definition of Gelatin you will better understand why.

"Gelatin. A brittle, nearly transparent, faintly yellow, odorless, and almost tasteless organic substance, obtained by boiling in water the ligaments, bones, skin, etc., of animals, and forming the basis of substances, as jellies, glues, and the like."

We can't help but wonder what the "etc." in this definition includes. But just what is listed is enough to turn your stomach. And how about the "glue" portion? It could well do that to your insides, just as the casein in milk, which makes one of the best known glues.

Perhaps this dictionary definition of glue might cause you to pause and think:

"An impure gelatin obtained by boiling skins, hoofs and other animal substances in water, and used for various purposes in the arts, especially as an adhesive medium in uniting substances."

This shows why we have to be constantly educating our minds with study so we know what to avoid and what is safe and healthful to eat.

In using Agar-Agar it is somewhat tricky to use, as it acts a little different than Gelatin. After the Agar-Agar is dissolved in hot water (use directions on package) add it to the pudding, pie or other ingredients at once, because it jells very fast, and sometimes it forms lumps. It is a good idea to add to the ingredients and blend together. It is much better to use a double boiler when dissolving the Agar-Agar.

———————

Meat eaters are usually staunch advocates of flesh foods. But I wonder how much they would really eat if they had to slaughter their own animals. Have you ever gone through a slaughter house and had to almost hold your nose to keep the stench from overcoming your sense of smell? Have you ever heard the wailing of the cattle being led to slaughter? Have you ever considered while drooling over a juicy steak you are at the same time digesting all the pain, fear and anger of the dying animal whose carcass you are devouring? Think about it the next time you cut into that rare prime rib.

FRUIT AND NUT CAKE

1/2 cup of soy flour
3/4 cups of sunflower seed meal (or grind sunflower seeds in nut mill)
1 cup of wheat flakes
1 cup of oatmeal
2 teaspoons of kelp
1 teaspoon of cinnamon
1/2 teaspoon of nutmeg
1 cup of dry coconut
1 cup of whole almonds
1/2 cup of whole sunflower seeds
1/2 cup of whole pecans
1/2 cup of peanuts (unsalted)
1/4 cup of sesame seeds
Mix dry ingredients
In separate bowl mix the following:
1/2 cup of honey
4 tablespoons of olive oil
1 tablespoon of vanilla
4 tablespoons of water
1/2 cup of currants
1/2 cup of almond nut butter or peanut butter
1/2 cup of raisins
1/2 cup of dates

(continued)

Grind the raisins and dates through a food grinder and add to honey mixture. Mix together and add to dry ingredients. Form into a loaf. Wrap in wax paper and keep in refrigerator.

SPICE CAKE

1/2 cup of soy flour
1/2 cup of sunflower seed meal (sunflower seeds can be used by putting them in the nut mill)
1 cup of wheat flakes or wheat germ
1 cup of oatmeal
2 teaspoons of kelp
1 teaspoon of cinnamon
1/2 teaspoon of nutmeg
1/2 teaspoon of ginger
1/2 cup of dry ground coconut
Mix dry ingredients together
In separate bowl mix the following:
1/4 cup of honey
3 tablespoons of olive oil
1 teaspoon of vanilla
3 tablespoons of water
1/2 cup of peanut butter or almond nut butter
Grind through food grinder:
1/2 cup of raisins
1/2 cup of dates
Mix ground fruit with honey mixture then mix with dry ingredients

(continued)

Put everything through food grinder second time. This is important. It makes a fine texture and mixes better if everything is put through the food grinder. Form into a loaf and press together into a firm loaf. Wrap in wax paper and store in refrigerator.

CHEESE CAKE

3 cups of soy cottage cheese (see recipe for soy cheese on page 86)
1/2 cup of honey
2 teaspoons of kelp
1 teaspoon of vanilla
1 tablespoon of lemon juice

Mix together and put into glass pie plate. Top with fresh cherries or pineapple. Sweeten with honey. Drain off liquid from fruit before putting on cheese cake. The honey makes the fruit juicy.

CHRISTMAS FRUIT CAKE

2 cups of pitted dates
2 cups of raisins
1 cup of currants
1 cup of prunes, pitted
1 cup of dried apricots

(continued)

1 cup of sesame seeds
1 cup of sunflower seeds
1 cup of shredded coconut
1 cup of almonds
1 cup of cashews
1/2 cup of honey
4 tablespoons of olive oil
1 cup of oatmeal

Mix pitted dates, raisins, currants, chopped apricots and prunes. Grind sesame seeds and sunflower seeds. Add to fruit mixture. Add shredded coconut. Add coarsely chopped almonds and cashews. Add honey, olive oil and oatmeal. Mix together well. Press in pan lined with wax paper or press in glass baking dish. Brush top with grape juice. Cover with wax paper. Store in refrigerator to season. Can be stored several days before serving.

———————

Did you ever know that man's original food is specified for him in the Bible?

"And God said, Behold, I have given you every herb bearing seed, which is upon the face of all the earth, and every tree, in the which is the fruit of a tree yielding seed; to you it shall be for meat." (The word "meat" is generic and means "food.") If the live food regime laid out in this verse had been followed, the history of the world would have been far different.

PEANUT BUTTER OATMEAL COOKIES

2 cups of dates (measure after pitted)
2 cups of raisins
1/2 cup of peanut butter
1/2 cup of ground peanuts (unsalted)
1 teaspoon of vanilla
1/2 cup of soy flour
1 cup of oatmeal
1/2 cup of wheat flakes
4 tablespoons of olive oil
2 tablespoons of water
Wheat germ

Put dates and raisins through food grinder and mix with other ingredients, except the wheat germ.

Mix in enough wheat germ until the dough is stiff.

Mix together and run through food grinder. This mixes the ingredients together and makes it more like a dough.

Roll out on wax paper, using soy flour to keep from sticking. Cut into cookie shapes and let dry for about an hour before storing in refrigerator. Use any of the frostings. See page 113 for recipes. Finely ground nuts or sunflower seeds can be sprinkled over top.

SPICE COOKIES

Use the recipe for peanut butter cookies. Substitute almond nut butter in place of peanut butter. Add:
1 teaspoon of cinnamon
1/4 teaspoon of nutmeg
1/2 teaspoon of ginger
Prepare the same as the peanut butter cookies.

CAROB COOKIES

Use the peanut butter cookie recipe. Substitute almond nut butter in place of peanut butter. Add 5 teaspoons of carob flour. Prepare the same as the peanut butter cookies.

DATE FILLED COOKIES

Use the peanut butter cookie recipe. Substitute almond nut butter in place of peanut butter, or you can use peanut butter if you want the peanut flavor. Roll out in thin layer. Cut out cookies. Fill with a mixture of date filling.
Date filling:
Mash dates or put through food grinder. Add a little water, about 2 tablespoons, to 2 cups of dates. Add soy flour and 1 tablespoon
(continued)

of honey. Mixture should be stiff. Cut out cookies. Add a teaspoon of date filling and cover with another cookie. Press edges. Store in refrigerator.

GINGER COOKIES

1/2 cup of corn meal
1/2 cup of wheat flakes
1/2 cup of wheat germ
1 cup of oatmeal
1 cup of pitted dates
3 teaspoons of kelp
2 tablespoons of honey
4 tablespoons of oil
1/2 teaspoon of ginger

Mix together. Put dates through food grinder. Add to other ingredients. Use just enough water to form a soft dough. Roll out 1/2 inch thick. Cut with cookie cutter and top with sesame seed frosting or carob frosting. This makes 1 doz. cookies.

When the blood stream is clogged with mucus it lowers the vital force in the body. You become sluggish and all dragged out. It's comparable to the friction created by a dirty engine or driving your car with the brakes on. Fruits loosen this mucus, creating a "fever," Nature's method of house cleaning.

FROSTINGS

SESAME SEED FROSTING

3 tablespoons of soy flour
3 teaspoons of sesame seeds
2 teaspoons of honey
1/2 teaspoon of vanilla
Enough water to make a thick paste. Then spread on cookies or cake.

CAROB FROSTING

3 tablespoons of soy flour
2 teaspoons of carob flour
2 teaspoons of honey
1/2 teaspoon of vanilla
Enough water to make a thick paste. Then spread on cookies or cake.

PEANUT BUTTER FROSTING

1/2 cup of peanut butter
3 teaspoons of olive or cooking oil
1/2 cup of honey
1 teaspoon of vanilla
Mix together. Spread on cakes or cookies.

APRICOT FROSTING

1 cup of apricots
1 teaspoon of vanilla
1/2 cup of soy flour
        Apricot or apple juice or water to make a paste for spreading. Use on cakes or cookies.

VANILLA FROSTING

3 tablespoons of soy flour
2 teaspoons of honey
1 teaspoon of vanilla
        Use enough water to make a thick paste. Spread on cake or cookies. Colored coconut can be sprinkled on top. See recipes for colored coconut under CONFECTIONS.

LEMON-ORANGE FROSTING

1 cup of soy flour
3/4 cup of honey
1 tablespoon of olive oil
1 teaspoon of grated orange rind
2 tablespoons of lemon juice
Orange juice
        Mix together and add enough orange juice for desired consistency. Use for cakes and cookies.

The puddings are made of fresh or frozen fruit. You can use the fruit of your choice or whatever is in season. I chose apricots for the butterscotch and peaches for the carob. These fruits are a good substitute for these flavors, and also they are available all year, fresh or frozen. Some of the fruits that can be used are: Papaya, pineapple, peaches, apricots, berries (most kinds). The banana is used in most of the recipes because it is used to thicken the pudding. Use your own imagination and see what a delicious pudding you can make. Most of these puddings provide good nutritious baby food.

PERSIMMON PUDDING
(Christmas season fruit)

3 persimmons
2 bananas
1/4 cup of honey

Liquefy together. If you like a thick smooth texture you can use a little almond nut butter. It is also a good food for this season of the year.

BUTTERSCOTCH PUDDING

2 cups of fresh or frozen apricots
2 bananas
6 tablespoons of honey
1 teaspoon of vanilla
1/4 cup of almond nut butter
Enough fig juice to liquefy to make a thick pudding. Serve with fresh grated coconut.

CAROB-NUT PUDDING

2 cups of fresh or frozen peaches
2 bananas
6 tablespoons of honey
1 teaspoon of vanilla
1/2 cup of coarsely ground nuts (almonds, cashews or pecans)
1/4 cup of almond nut butter (optional)
Liquefy together with enough prune juice to make a thick pudding. The nut butter makes a thick smooth texture. Serve plain or with grated coconut.

PARFAIT

Fill chilled parfait glasses with 1/3 glass of butterscotch pudding. Slice bananas or straw-
(continued)

berries to fill 1/3 of glass. Finish filling with carob pudding. Top with coconut or serve plain. Other puddings and fruits can be substituted. Use fruits that are in season, and also the puddings of your choice.

PERSIMMON PUDDING
(With frozen fruit cubes)

Use enough frozen apricot or peach cubes to make 2 cups. (See recipe for frozen cubes under JAMS AND BUTTERS.) Put in blender. Add:
1/4 cup of honey
1 large persimmon
Blend until well blended. If cubes are not available, use frozen fruits. Since persimmons are a winter fruit, about Christmas time it is easier to use frozen fruits. Fresh fruits are not always available at that season of the year.

CAROB PUDDING

2 cups of water
1/4 cup of soy flour
1/2 cup of sunflower seeds
4 tablespoons of carob
1/2 cup of pitted dates
1 tablespoon of vanilla
Blend together until smooth.

VARIATIONS

CAROB FRUIT PUDDING

Substitute 2 cups of fruit in place of 2 cups of water.

VANILLA PUDDING

Substitute 2 cups of fruit in place of 2 cups of water. Omit carob.

LEMON CHIFFON PUDDING

1/2 cup of honey
1/4 cup of lemon juice
1/4 cup of almond nut butter
1 tablespoon of vegetable Gelatin
1/2 cup of cold water
1/2 cup of hot water
2 cups of finely chopped apples
Liquefy all ingredients except Gelatin and water. Dissolve Gelatin in cold water until jelled. When jelled add hot water to dissolve. Add to the ingredients in blender. Liquefy. Chill in blender. When jelled liquefy 2 or 3 seconds to make fluffy. Pour into desert dishes.

This exotic tropical fruit is not too easy to come by, but if you do live near an area where you can get it, by all means do so. If ever there were a miracle fruit, this is it. We live not far from the Mexican border, and we regularly have gone to the markets there and procured it. Recently we found a man who makes periodic trips to and from Mexico and brings back much of this glorious fruit. So now we buy from him and save ourselves a lot of unnecessary travel.

Dr. B. Lytton-Bernard, D.Sc., D.O., has a health spa at Guadalajara, Mexico, and he is an enthusiastic advocate of the papaya as an indispensable part of his therapeutic practice. He says that the papayain enzyme has the power of digesting 300 times its volume of protein, and that he has yet to find a more effective cleansing agent. He says it cleans not only the alimentary canal but reaches all the tissues. He believes that in the papaya lies the key to rejuvenating the body to such a degree that life can be greatly prolonged, and without diminished faculties.

Papaya is a melon that should not be eaten until it gets soft. In Mexico they serve papaya with lemon or lime juice. In many tropical countries they eat papaya with other fruits like pineapple. In Florida they like papaya with cottage cheese, which of course we do not recommend except for those on a transition diet. We do not believe any milk product is fit for human consumption. You can make papaya aspic by cutting it up, blending it in your blender, adding lemon or lime juice, and putting in your refrigerator to jell. It is delicious this way. However you prepare it, be sure to eat as much papaya as you can get. You can never eat too much of this fruit of the gods.

One of the commonest complaints we hear when we tell people we live mostly on fruit is: "Where in the world do you get enough protein?" On a live food regime you don't have to worry about protein, starches or fats. Mother Nature has already taken care of that problem for us by incorporating in the raw foods all the elements we need for bodily health. When you eat live foods you won't have to worry about unnaturally putting on weight, for example. For live foods are not fattening, not even avocados or bananas. If you are over-weight, you will automatically lose; if you are under-weight, you will automatically gain -- to the norm Nature intended for you when she formed the matrix of your body in your mother's womb.

APRICOT SHERBERT

2 cups of frozen apricots (slightly soft)
2 frozen bananas
1 cup of orange juice or fruit juice (enough juice to liquefy the fruit)
1 teaspoon of vanilla
Honey to sweeten

Put frozen fruit in blender and liquefy with juice, honey and vanilla until thick like sherbert. It is easy to peel the bananas if you put them under the cold water faucet and peel with a knife. Cut in slices and add to fruit in blender. Put in container and keep in freezer until ready to serve. Should not be in freezer very long because it will crystallize. Should be made just before ready to serve. Any kind of frozen fruit can be used in place of the apricots. A mixture of apricots and pineapple or peaches is very good.

APRICOT ICE CREAM

Use recipe for apricot sherbert, only use 1/2 cup of almond nut butter and more frozen bananas. The nut butter and bananas give it a texture like ice cream. For a special treat, serve coconut whip cream on top.

COCONUT ICE CREAM

2 cups of frozen fruit:
Apricots, peaches, pineapple or a mixture of any three
1/2 cup of almond nut butter
1 cup of coconut whipped cream
3 frozen bananas
1 teaspoon of vanilla
Enough fruit juice to liquefy
Honey to sweeten

Liquefy in blender until thick like ice cream.

CAROB ICE CREAM

4 cups of frozen apricots
3 frozen bananas
1/2 cup of honey
3/4 cup of almond nut butter
1 teaspoon of vanilla
4 teaspoons of carob
Prune juice

Liquefy in blender, using enough prune juice to liquefy. If this is not frozen enough after liquefying, put in freezer and freeze, but do not allow to crystallize. Fudge sickles can be made by putting a Popsickle stick in mixture before freezing in sickles.

BASIC ICE CREAM
(Large amount)

5 cups of water
2 cups of soy flour
3/4 cups of honey
1/2 cup of olive oil
1 tablespoon of vanilla
3 cups of fruit (any flavor you desire)

     Blend together and pour into ice cube trays. When frozen, remove cubes and put in plastic bags. Store in freezer. When ready to serve ice cream put a few cubes in blender with a small amount of water or juice. Blend until consistency of ice cream. A Popsickle stick can be placed in the basic ice cream mixture before freezing in cubes of Popsickles.

STRAWBERRY ICE CREAM

2 cups of frozen or fresh strawberries
4 cups of water
1/2 cup of honey
1/2 cup of almond nut butter
1 cup of soy flour
1/2 cup of olive oil
1 cup of papaya or other kind of fruit

     Blend together and freeze in ice cube trays or freezer. Popsickles can be made by putting Popsickle sticks in mixture before freezing into cubes.

PEACH ICE CREAM

2 cups of frozen peaches
1 cup of apple juice
3 frozen bananas
1/2 cup of almond nut butter
4 tablespoons of honey
1 teaspoon of vanilla

Put apple juice, honey, vanilla and almond nut butter in blender. Add frozen bananas and frozen peaches until the mixture is stiff like ice cream. Serve at once. If you have to store this in the freezer before serving be sure to stir frequently and only keep in freezer for a short time, otherwise it will crystallize.

RAISIN-PECAN ICE CREAM

1 cup of water, pineapple juice or orange juice
1 cup of raisins
3/4 cups of pecans
2 frozen bananas
2 cups of frozen fruit

Use peaches, pineapple or apricots or a combination of these fruits. Put juice in blender. Add raisins and pecans, then blend. Add frozen fruit. Liquefy. If not stiff enough add more frozen fruit.

DATE BALLS

2 cups of dates
1 cup of raisins
1 cup of nuts (pecans, almonds, English walnuts or a mixture of them)
1/4 cup of coconut

      Pit dates. Put dates and raisins through food grinder. Chop nuts to medium size. Mix ingredients together. Make into balls. Roll in grated coconut or finely ground nuts. Keep in refrigerator.

STUFFED DATES

      Pit dates. Fill with whole pecans. Serve plain or cover with grated coconut.

DATE ROLL

2 cups of dates
1 cup of raisins
1 cup of nuts

(continued)

Put dates and raisins through food grinder. Chop nuts fine and add to dates and raisins. Roll out like a pie crust. Fill with grated coconut. Roll in long roll. Store in refrigerator. When ready to serve, slice in 3/4 inch slices.

CAROB FOR COATED NUTS & DATE BALLS

1 cup of water
1/2 cup of Agar-Agar. Steam in covered pan until dissolved. Then cool.
Mix 3/4 cup of carob flour
3 tablespoons of water
1/2 cup of honey
1/4 cup of molasses

Beat this mixture until well blended. Stir this mixture in the pan of Agar-Agar. Cover nuts and date balls. It is better to have the date balls and nuts cold before coating them with the carob.

APRICOT BALLS

2 cups of dried apricots
1 cup of nuts
1 cup of dates
1/4 cup of raisins

Put ingredients through food grinder and cover with ground coconut or carob coating.

FRUIT FUDGE BALLS

1-1/2 cups of raisins
1/2 cup of currants
1/2 cup of pecans

Put through food grinder. Form into small flat patties. Mix 1/4 cup of peanut butter with 2 tablespoons of lemon or lime juice and 1 tablespoon of honey. Spread top of patties with peanut butter mixture. Form into balls so that the peanut butter mixture will be in the middle of the balls. Mix 1/4 cup of soy flour, 3 tablespoons of honey, 3 tablespoons of carob flour, 1 teaspoon of vanilla and enough water to make a thick paste. Spread balls with carob mixture and roll into the balls so that each ball will have a thick coating of the carob mixture. Roll in ground coconut or ground nuts.

DATE SQUARES

2 cups of oatmeal
1/2 cup of soy flour
1/2 cup of sesame seed ground fine
1/4 cup of honey
4 tablespoons of olive oil
1 cup of sunflower seeds ground fine

(continued)

Mix together. Divide in half. Crumble half the mixture in a glass baking dish and press to cover bottom of dish. Fill with date filling. Crumble other half over top and press down. Cut in squares.

DATE FILLING

2 cups of pitted dates
1/2 cup of almond nut butter
1/2 cup of soy flour
1 cup of coarsely ground nuts (pecans or cashews are good to use)

Soak pitted dates in small amount of warm water to soften. Add almond nut butter and soy flour. If mixture is too thick, add a little water or prune juice.

CAROB FUDGE

2/3 cup of carob
1 cup of dates
2 tablespoons of soy flour
1-1/4 cups of water
2 tablespoons of Agar-Agar
1 tablespoon of vanilla
1/2 cup of nuts (your favorite kind)

(continued)

Dissolve Agar-Agar in water in the top of double boiler. Pit dates and cut in pieces. Add other ingredients and mix. Add Agar-Agar and stir well. Pour into square dish. Chill. Cut in squares.

OATMEAL-NUT CANDY

1 cup of rolled oatmeal
1/2 cup of carob
1/4 cup of ground sesame seeds
1/4 cup of ground sunflower seeds
1/2 cup of honey
1 cup of broken nuts (your favorite kind)

Mix by hand. Roll in bars. Cover with carob coating. These can be stored in freezer.

COLORED COCONUT

1 pint of finely ground coconut from health food store or specialty food store
1 tablespoon of prickly pear juice or
1 tablespoon of beet juice

Put juice and coconut in jar and shake until coconut is colored. Spread on cookie sheet and put in oven (low heat) to dry. Use to cover candies or sprinkle top of cake and cookies. For green color, use juice of parsley. (Run the parsley in nut mill, then press out juice.) For orange color, use carrot juice.

DATE-NUT BARS

1-1/2 cups of soy flour
1/2 cup of sunflower seeds (ground fine)
1/2 cup of sesame seeds (ground fine)
1/2 cup of pecans (ground fine)
1 teaspoon of kelp
8 tablespoons of honey
4 tablespoons of peanut butter
1/2 cup of water
1 cup of ground dates

Mix together. Press or roll on wax paper. Cut into bars. Cover with carob coating.

One of the biggest bugaboos of the raw food movement is proper combinations of foods. Here again we meet the old familiar problem of conflicting authorities. And once again you have to resolve the conflict to your own satisfaction in the crucible of YOUR experience, not someone else's. Doesn't it seem rather odd for us to fret over proper combinations when Nature herself doesn't? For instance, if you don't eat fats and proteins at the same meal, how can you eat eggs, which consist of 6.7% protein and 5.2% fat? Or soybeans, which contain 13.2% protein, 13.6% starch and 6.3% fat? The list is a long one. The one cardinal rule which most authorities agree on is: eat fruits and vegetables separately. Don't mix them at one meal.

NEW YEAR

Breakfast:
Apples, raisins with peanut butter cream
Carob cup

Noon Meal:
Cream of onion soup
Mock Shrimp Louie with tartar sauce
Shredded turnips
Relish tray
Imitation rye bread with date butter
Mint tea
Cheese cake

Supper:
Broth soup
Warm potato salad
Corn bread with date butter

VALENTINE'S DAY

Noon Meal:
Fathmanburgers with tomato sauce
Shredded beets with lemon-oil dressing
Shredded turnips with lemon-oil dressing or
mayonnaise
Nut oatmeal bread with fig or date butter
Lemon chiffon pudding

EASTER

Noon Meal:
Mock salmon loaf with tartar sauce
Peas and carrot croquettes with curry sauce
Tossed green salad
Butterscotch pie

JULY 4th

Noon Meal:
Vegetable salad
Stuffed tomatoes
Shredded beets with lemon-oil dressing
Shredded turnips with lemon-oil dressing
Apricot ice cream

Supper:
Summer fruit salad
Ginger cookies

LABOR DAY

Noon Meal:
Avocado croquettes
Carrot and raisin salad
Succotash a la Koobatian
Cornbread #2 with apricot butter
Coconut ice cream

THANKSGIVING

Breakfast:
Apple-banana with almond nut butter cream

Noon Meal:
Onion soup
Mock turkey
Carrot loaf with curry sauce
Salad (lettuce with tomato dressing)
Peas and carrot croquettes
Cranberry sauce
Fruit cake or mince pie with cinnamon sauce
Mint tea

CHRISTMAS

Breakfast:
Applesauce
Sliced bananas

Noon Meal:
Avocado soup
Chicken a la Cheryl
Cabbage salad
Relish tray
Cranberry sauce
Broccoli patties with tomato sauce
Fruit cake or mince pie with cinnamon sauce or
persimmon pudding

BIRTHDAY

Noon Meal:
Mock tuna fish with tartar sauce
Stuffed tomatoes
Stuffed avocado
Green bean salad
Spice cake or cheese cake

COMPANY

Noon Meal:
Cream of onion soup
Mexican guacamole
Relish tray
Carob pudding

SUNDAY

Noon Meal:
Vichysoisse or pea soup
Tossed green salad
Mock Crab Louie with tartar sauce
Imitation chocolate pie

Supper:
Fruit salad
Date-filled cookies

<u>Buffet:</u>
Relish tray
Fruit tray
Stuffed peppers
Stuffed avocados
Stuffed tomatoes
Carob rye bread
Rye bread
Date and fig butter
Confections

SCHOOL LUNCH

<u>Lettuce and peanut butter sandwiches</u>
Mix a little mayonnaise with peanut butter. Spread on lettuce leaf. Top with another lettuce leaf and roll into a roll. Wrap in wax paper.

<u>Apple and date sandwiches</u>
Core and slice apples. Spread with peanut butter and dates or date butter.

<u>Carrot loaf</u>
Use recipe for carrot loaf. Put in glass jar to fit lunch box.

Fruit that is in season, confections, cake and cookies.

(continued on next page)

(continued on next page)

MUCUSLESS DIET HEALING SYSTEM (194 pages, 24 lessons)
A complete usable program by Arnold Ehret explains in plain,
easily understood language the Ehret teachings.

RATIONAL FASTING for PHYSICAL, MENTAL AND
Spiritual REJUVENATION. This thought provoking book
by Arnold Ehret has aided thousands to enjoy health through
fasting. It also includes "Your Road to Regeneration" by
Arnold Ehret, "My Road to Health" and "Build Your Own
Road to Health" by Teresa Mitchell, "Internal Cleanliness" by
Fred S. Hirsch and The Definite Cure of Chronic Constipation
by Arnold Ehret.

THE CAUSE AND CURE OF HUMAN ILLNESS (Kranke
Menschen) by Arnold Ehret. Translated by Professor Dr.
Ludwig Max Fischer. A way to take your health back into
your own hands. A solutions to mans modern ailments. It
was proposed and articulated by a nutritionist, Arnold Ehret,
in a book written one hundred years ago.

PAMPHLETS ON EHRETS TEACHINGS

THUS SPEAKETH THE STOMACH also THE TRAGEDY OF
NUTRITION.

PHYSICAL FITNESS THRU A SUPERIOR DIET, FASTING
and DIETETICS.

OTHER BOOKS OF INTEREST

THE GRAPE CURE by Johanna Brandt. The author offers her personal contribution toward the solution of the Cancer problem and her personal experiences in overcoming this dreaded ailment. This book is intended more as a Cancer preventive.

The Ehret Literature Publishing Company, Inc.
P O Box 24
Dobbs Ferry, New York 10522-0024
www.arnoldehret.org